Westward to the Pacific

An Overview of America's Westward Expansion

Ray Allen Billington

Design: Massimo Vignelli

Contents

Foreword

There are times when history seems to gain momentum, when separate streams join and accelerate. Then events tumble after one another and people—ordinary people—suddenly are faced with new challenges. Such periods are times of tremendous energy and change, with liberal doses of genuine drama. Later generations looking back may feel envy, and even historians may find it difficult to separate remembered romance from fact—which often turn out to be two facets of the same event.

The 19th Century in the American West was such a time. There was wonder and discovery. There was conflict between nations, between groups and between individuals. The century opened with the Lewis & Clark Expedition feeling its way into an unknown vastness, at mid-century railroads were appearing, and at century's end there were interior cities tearing down "old" buildings to replace them with new. Change came at a dizzy pace. It may not have seemed so to a pioneer plodding his ox-pace way west over the quiet, endless prairie, or to a sod-buster on his lonely farm, working through a dry, sunny afternoon and fearing a hundred more before the drought broke or the banker came. But a mere listing of some of the themes of that century shows the compression of events that took place, and hints at ten thousand human experiences: Explorers, Mountain Men, Steamboats, the Santa Fe Trail, Pioneer Wagon Trains, the War with Mexico, the Gold Rush!, the Pony Express, Stagecoaches, Indian Wars, Railroads, Cowboys, Outlaws, Sod-busters... and old people remembering.

In order to reach a wider audience with the story of America's westward expansion, the Jefferson National Expansion Historical Association is publishing **The Gateway Series** *of books for the general reader. Each will be a fresh telling of some phase of that tremendous story. Authors are being selected who are noted not only for their accuracy, but also for their ability to tell the story well. No pulp fiction here; there is no gain, and some loss, in distorting our own heritage.*

2

Ray Allen Billington was an obvious choice to write an essay to open the series. Dr. Billington is the dean of historians of the American West. He has taught at several major American universities, as well as Oxford. Perhaps his most influential book is the text **Westward Expansion.** *(It certainly was influential to this editor, who studied it in college!) Other major works include* **America's Frontier Heritage,** *the biography* **Frederick Jackson Turner: Historian, Scholar, Teacher,** *and (with Martin Ridge)* **America's Frontier Story,** *which is an annotated compilation of the documentary rock from which good history is carved. His articles are too numerous to list. He is a founder and past-president of the Western History Association (as well as numerous other professional organizations), and is now the Senior Research Associate at the Huntington Library.*

History is fascinating at the level of stories of human experience. It becomes useful as well as fascinating when past experiences are combined and compared, so they can give us insights into our own situation. From his lifetime of thinking about America's westering experience Dr. Billington points out ways it has helped form both the good and the troublesome of our national character, and identifies some implications for the future.

This is important reading with an icing: it is **good** *reading.*

Dan Murphy, Editor

The Frontiering Experience

If the scores of travelers from overseas who visited the United States during the nineteenth and early twentieth centuries are to be believed, we Americans are all slightly mad. We refuse to pay proper respect to those of superior lineage, insist on calling each other "Gentlemen" or "Ladies" whatever our origins, and pridefully bestow the reigns of government on the humble and undeserving. We are blatantly nationalistic, boasting endlessly of our democratic institutions, and sometimes flexing our military muscles uselessly when another nation indulges in a bit of diplomatic game-playing. We are always experimenting with new ideas and gadgets, even though the old are still useful. We are forever moving about, shifting from house to house and state to state, and squandering so much vacation time on travel that we have no time for enjoyment when we arrive. We work endlessly, and seem unable to enjoy true leisure. We are so shamefully wasteful that our machines are cunningly contrived for premature obsolescence; one traveler compared the American home to a reverse assembly line, deliberately reducing to rubble the gadgets with which it is plentifully stocked. We worship the Almighty Dollar beyond all reason, treat our wives with a respect no European woman could expect, and are so optimistic that we would refuse to recognize the Day of Doom were its shadow already upon us.

Whence came these differences so universally noted by visitors? No one answer to that question can suffice, of course. The "national character"—if indeed we have one—is rooted in the multitude of molding forces that shaped the American people during the nation's formative years: the lack of a medieval tradition to serve as a brake on innovation; the contributions of a variety of cultures as immigrants from many nations met and mingled; the rapidity of the transition from a rural to an industrialized society; the abundance of natural resources and the resulting high living standard; and many more. All contributed to our "national character," but all leave something to be desired as a satisfactory explanation for the differences between our culture and Europe's.

We may find a clue to a more convincing explanation by recognizing that the traits isolated by visitors as most unique appeared in most exaggerated form along the frontiers—in the successive Wests that the

6

British statesman, Lord Bryce, called "the most American part of America." The mere process of frontiering, apparently, generated and intensified the characteristics and institutions that differentiated Americans from their Old World ancestors. Something was happening at that point where civilization entered the wilderness in the three-century-long conquest of the continent, something that transformed Europeans into Americans. What was this mysterious alchemy, and how did it affect this transformation?

In seeking to answer that question, we must remember that westering was a process that was repeated over and over again for three hundred years—between the first settlements at James Town and Plymouth and Massachusetts Bay in the early seventeenth century, to the exhaustion of the public domain in the twentieth. Over and over again during those centuries pioneers moved into virgin lands, discarding some of their cultural baggage each time they did so. Complex governmental controls were unnecessary in sparsely settled frontier communities and were replaced by simple associations of settlers; economic specialization was impossible when each pioneer cared for the needs of his own family, and gave way to primitive systems of barter; cultural outpourings were outmoded in a land where hard physical labor was essential to tame a wilderness. So the frontiersmen discarded the practices and institutions of the compact Easts they had left behind. The discarding was reluctant, for their one hope was to reproduce those practices as rapidly as possible; but discard them they did.

Then, gradually as more and more settlers flocked in, that pioneer community climbed back toward civilization and a matured social order. The new social order, however, differed from that of the East on which it was modeled. It had been altered by the cultural contributions of settlers from differing backgrounds, by the variations inevitable in separate evolutions, and above all by the unique social environment of the frontier. For there, where virgin resources were waiting exploitation, where an individual's ancestry was less important than his skills, and where no entrenched elite blocked the path to wealth and prestige, the individual was free to climb as high on the social ladder as his energy and ambition could carry him. To the ordinary American or immigrant, with an abundance of hope and ability but little else, the frontier was the land of opportunity. There he could escalate to wealth and prestige as he could not in the stabilized Easts. This was the unique feature of the American frontier, which more than any other helps explain the distinctive qualities of the nation's people.

All Americans during the three centuries of westering *believed* (whether rightly or wrongly makes no difference) that by moving to the frontier they could better themselves economically and socially. This faith in the availability of opportunity for all altered their attitudes toward their fellow men and toward society. It did this whether they chose to go west themselves or not, but most radically among those who did go. This was inevitable. A small farmer in Massachusetts who was certain that he could make his fortune by moving to newly opened lands in western New York was sure to see life differently from a German peasant who was bound forever to his small plot by poverty and feudal dues.

Frontier opportunity, then—the chance to "grow up with the country" in the phrase of that day— reshaped the social attitudes of frontiersmen and all Americans. Their faith in political democracy was rekindled; rule by the elite was outmoded in a land where all were landholders, where local problems were unique and demanded local solutions, and where a lower class had been outlawed by the abundance of nature's resources. Their faith in social democracy was also rekindled. Distinctions between classes were hard to maintain on a frontier where a turn of a miner's shovel or a fortunate land speculation might make the village pauper the richest, and hence most respected, citizen. In such a social order ancestry could hardly be important. "We don't vally those things in this country," one visitor was told. "It's what's above ground, not what's under, that we think on." In that atomized society all men were future "gentlemen" and deserved this designation, all women were prospective "ladies" and should be treated as such. "With us," one frontiersman stoutly maintained, "a man's a man, whether he have a silk gown on him or not."

The belief in opportunity that affected this transformation helped generate other traits that struck visitors as peculiarly American—and that were also products of frontiering. One was the uncontrollable compulsion of the pioneers to move on, and on, and on. Ahead of them, always ahead, danced the will-o'-the-wisp of illusive fortune: the untrapped beaver stream, the vein of gold ore, the fortunate land speculation. "If hell lay to the west," wrote one observer, "they would cross heaven to reach it." Most eventually settled down to enjoy the degree of prosperity to which their abilities entitled them, but others drifted throughout their lives, always in hope. Clarence King, the geologist, met such a family, the Newtys, in California's Sierra; they had shifted from Missouri to Oregon, from Oregon to California, and were about to depart for Montana with their sole possessions: three thousand hogs. Dirty, illiterate, miserable, Ma and Pa and innumerable children crowded into a single bed, they were, as King put it, part of that "dreary brotherhood of perpetual emigrants who roam as dreary waifs over the West." Little matter. No number of failures could dim their hope. This was the frontier dream, and the American dream.

From it stemmed a whole gallery of American eccentricities that observers loved to cite. The frontiersmen were ruthlessly wasteful, slashing away the forests, grubbing out the mineral wealth, slaughtering the wildlife, robbing the soil of its fertility—all with no thought of the future. If reminded of posterity, they would answer, "What has posterity done for me?" Pioneers felt no need to conserve natural resources or to preserve the beauty of the countryside; moving on to an unexploited and unspoiled landscape was cheaper and easier. "Why son," a Nebraska pioneer boasted, "by the time I was your age I had wore out three farms." Here today and gone tomorrow; let the future care for itself.

Their faith in the future converted frontiersmen into incurable optimists, living not amidst the half-cleared fields and poverty of the present, but in a future where fortune had smiled. They were compulsive workers, for incessant labor was necessary if they were to conquer the forests and plains as their ambition demanded. Immigrants from Europe complained that they were expected to do three days work in one in the West. Work was a social duty, as essential to the welfare of the community as it was to the individual. Those who shirked were either driven out or "hated out" of the settlement. The necessities of

To early westerners the natural resources of the West seemed inexhaustible, the virgin timber stands endless; so why conserve? Photo by Darius Kinsey: Courtesy Culver Pictures

pioneering similarly glorified the practical at the expense of the aesthetic, just as they demanded ingenuous solutions to many unique problems in a land where each individual had to care for his own needs. The pioneer who was seen to repair a broken harness by taking off his britches, stuffing them with grass, fitting them about the horse's neck, and continuing plowing in his long-johns typified the inventive spirit necessary on frontiers.

To say that these traits and others like them were solely the product of the frontiering experience would be to oversimplify the complexity of the past. All were rooted in the Old World heritage, and all were modified by the variety of forces that operated during the nation's formative years. Yet frontiering did play a major role in accentuating those characteristics and institutions judged most uniquely American by observers from overseas. If we are to understand ourselves, and be a good neighbor in a shrinking world, we must understand our pioneer past. The purpose of this book is not only to trace the history of westward expansion, but to help explain why we behave as Americans.

Fourth of July crowd at
Gateway Arch, St. Louis.
Photo by Joseph Matthews:
Courtesy Jefferson National
Expansion Memorial

Conquering the Mississippi Valley

Lake Superior

Lake Huron

Lake Michigan

Milwaukee

Rock R.

Chicago

✕ **Thames**
Detroit
Fort Malden □ ✕ **Put-In Bay**
Lake Erie

Fallen Timbers ✕

✕ **Tippecanoe**

NATIONAL **ROAD**

Pittsburgh

Ohio
River

Louisville

Kentucky R.

St. Louis

Mississippi River

Cumberland Gap

L. Ontario

ERIE CANAL

Buffalo

Mohawk
Valley

Hudson R.

Plymouth

Boston

New Amsterdam
(New York)

APPALACHIAN MTS.

Cumberland

Potomac R.

WILDERNESS ROAD

James Town

ATLANTIC OCEAN

Horseshoe Bend ✕

S P A N I S H   F L O R I D A
(until 1819)

New Orleans

G U L F   O F   M E X I C O

**The Expansion of the
American People Begins**
Map by Harry Scott

Fort □
Battle Site ✕
State Boundary —·—

| 0 | | 100 | | 200 Miles |
| 0 | 100 | 200 | | 300 Kilometers |

Westering was their way of life. Their grand-fathers had moved out from Europe's beachheads at James Town and New Amsterdam, out from Ply-mouth and Boston, out over the coastal lowlands to plant their farms along the river bottoms at first, then in the highlands between. Their fathers had overrun the hilly Appalachian foothills and spilled over into the Great Valley of the Appalachians, there to mingle with a southward-moving stream of pioneers from Pennsylvania composed largely of Scots-Irish from Ulster and Germans from the Rhinish Palatinate—the "Pennsylvania Dutch." They themselves had breached the mountain barrier to plant their wilder-ness outposts along the upper Ohio, along the westward-flowing Watauga and Nolichucky and Cumberland rivers of Tennessee, and in the lush blue-grass country of Kentucky. Now, in the years just after the Revolutionary War, their sons were itching to be on the move once more, ever westward, to begin the conquest of the broad Mississippi Valley.

They had learned much of frontiering since their ancestors had starved to death amidst nature's plenty at James Town and Plymouth. They knew how to gir-dle the trees by cutting a notch a few feet from the ground, to plant their first crop of Indian corn among the standing trunks, to cut away the dying forest monarchs and call in neighbors for a "log-rolling" that would pile them for burning, to build a zig-zagged "worm fence" of rails that would guard their fields from marauding cattle, to build the sturdy log cabins needed to house their growing families. Above all they had perfected the use of the two tools essential to frontiering in forested areas: the long-shafted ax that was the universal tool against nature, and the straight-barreled "Kentucky rifle" that brought down game and provided some protection against the Indians whose lands they wanted.

These skills were necessary, but so also was a new self-reliant spirit that set the pioneers off from their city-dwelling cousins. They were the "men of the western waters," and their destiny was to win a conti-nent for the infant republic of which they were so proud. Haughtily independent, recklessly disdainful of danger, confident of their own strength and con-temptuous of those less gifted in wilderness ways, they were ready to muscle their way westward—even to the Pacific. A journalist watched a backwoods hunter come striding into Philadelphia "with the step of Achilles," and saw in him "one of the progenitors of an unconquerable race"—"his face presented the traces of a spirit quick to resent—he had the will to dare, and the power to execute; there was something in his look which bespoke a disdain of control, and an absence of constraint in all his movements indicated an habitual independence of thought and action." Here was the sturdy stuff of which the pioneers were made.

The future was theirs now, and they were eager to make it their own. For a generation they had been held back by the fury of Indian attack during the Revolution and by the post-war diplomatic problems that had made the frontiers unsafe for a decade. Finally Jay's Treaty with England in 1794 and "Mad Anthony" Wayne's victory over the Indians at the Battle of Fallen Timbers a year later had brought temporary peace to the Great Lakes country. Then Thomas Pinckney's Treaty of San Lorenzo with Spain in 1795 ended Indian warfare in the Southwest and opened a market for westerners' produce by guaranteeing Americans the right to navigate the Mississippi River. By the mid-1790s the borderlands were safe, and the westward tide was ready to roll again.

All the ingredients for a major rush were there. In the East land worn thin by repeated plantings was escalating in price as population thickened; by 1795 rock-strewn farm lands in New England sold for twenty or thirty dollars an acre while proven tobacco lands in the Southeast fetched even more. In the (then) West land was abundant, and cheap. Much was owned by speculators who demanded a return on their investment, but competition between them kept prices reasonable and all were eager to sell on credit. More was owned by the federal government which after 1800 would charge a customer only $160 in cash for 320 choice acres, with another $480 due in four more years. Nor were these bargains hard to reach. By the 1790s crude "roads" stretched into the interior from Albany, Philadelphia and the Carolinas. Most of them were rutted horrors made by cutting the smaller trees, bridging a few streams with makeshift structures, and "corduroying" mudholes with a layer of small logs. But they led toward the setting sun and Eden was worth a few discomforts.

"Highways and Byeways of the Forest," George Tattersall. By 1790 roads were penetrating the interior and, although primitive by modern standards, led thousands to new homes. Courtesy Museum of Fine Arts, Boston

So the population tide began to flow, slowly at first, then with increased momentum into the 1800s. Roads were so jammed that stragglers were forced from the highways. Some emigrants were in wagons with family goods piled high, some on horseback, some on foot with all their worldly goods strapped to their backs, trudging through the snow of early spring "because everybody says it's good land." As the newcomers scattered through the backcountry all was bustle and hurrah: trees falling, cabins rising, the smoke from burning trees blueing the air. Wrote an observer in western New York: "The woods are full of new settlers. Axes are resounding, and the trees literally falling about us as we passed. In one instance we were obliged to pass in a field through the smoke and flames of the trees that had lately been felled and were just fired." The rush was on, fed by tales of bottomlands in the West that yielded one hundred bushels to the acre, and seemed destined to go on forever.

From the uplands of the Southeast came seasoned pioneers who made the river bottoms of eastern Tennessee their mecca, or followed Daniel Boone's Wilderness Road (cut through Cumberland Gap just before the Revolution) into the lush bluegrass country of Kentucky, and beyond. Kentucky became a state in 1792 and Tennessee four years later. From New England and New York another stream followed the Mohawk Valley westward to spread over western New York State, where Dutch and English speculators had improved vast tracts that they were eager to sell on credit. By 1812 two hundred thousand people lived in western New York, nearly all of them from New England. Other New Englanders leap-frogged beyond to Ohio which earned statehood in 1802, or Indiana whose territorial legislature met in 1805. Even distant Illinois counted thirteen thousand settlers in 1812 when its first territorial legislature met.

Each burst of expansion in the history of the frontier brought tragedy in its wake, and this was no exception. Every foot of land occupied by the pioneers had to be wrested from the Indians, usually by government agents who used fraud, deceit, and force to drive the Native Americans from their tribal homelands. For a time the red men were willing to yield rather than risk war, but as pressure upon them continued, they realized that they must make a stand

*"Daniel Boone Escorting
Settlers through the
Cumberland Gap." Boone
took his family across the
Appalachians in 1775.
Seventy-five years later
George Caleb Bingham, with
the continuing emigration
swirling around him in
Missouri, painted the event.
Undoubtedly Boone's crossing
was more crude and primitive
than portrayed, but Bingham's
painting reveals the epic
quality Americans saw in their
own westward movement.*
Courtesy Washington University
Gallery of Art, St. Louis

or face extermination. That realization led always to war and an inevitable outcome: defeat for the Indians and further plunder of their lands.

The agent of American aggression who touched off this cycle in the early nineteenth century was William Henry Harrison, an Indian-hating frontiersman who served as governor of Indiana Territory. In a series of treaties with corrupt chiefs or fragments of tribes, Harrison managed to acquire for the United States all of southern Indiana, most of southeastern Michigan, and a sizeable chunk of Illinois. Eventually the Indians found a leader who could challenge his ruthless tactics. Tecumseh, a Shawnee chief who combined shrewd intelligence with remarkable oratorical powers, saw that the red men could protect themselves only by forming a confederation of tribes with each pledged not to cede land unless he had the consent of all. This was the message that he and Tenskwatawa, or the Prophet, a one-eyed epileptic medicine-man thought to possess supernatural powers, began preaching. They had such success that by 1808 they had welded together an organization that seemed capable of halting Harrison's land-grabs. That year Tecumseh founded the village of Prophetstown on Tippecanoe Creek in Indiana as headquarters for his confederation. At about the same time he visited Fort Malden in Canada, where he was encouraged to believe that should war begin, the red coats (English) would fight on the side of the red men.

Blissfully unaware of these ominous developments, Harrison in 1809 negotiated the treaty of Fort Wayne with a fragment of a tribe not associated with the confederation, gaining some three million acres of choice Indiana land. Tecumseh wrathfully announced that any attempt to occupy the cession would lead to war. Raids began a year later and full-scale fighting in 1811 when the Shawnee leader visited the South to rally the nations there to his cause. "War now," he thundered to five thousand Creeks, Cherokees, and Choctaws gathered on the banks of the Tallapoosa River, "War forever. War upon the living. War upon the dead; dig up their very corpses from the graves; our country must give no rest to a white man's bones." While Tecumseh was rallying supporters, Harrison decided to take advantage of his absence by marching on Prophetstown. The Battle of

William Henry Harrison, whose success in acquiring Indian lands and victory at Tippecanoe led to the presidency. Daguerrotype by Southworth and Hawes: Courtesy Metropolitan Museum of Art

Tecumseh, remarkable Shawnee chief who formed a far-flung Indian coalition. Killed opposing Harrison at the battle of the Thames, 1813. Artist unknown: Courtesy Field Museum of Natural History, Chicago

Tenskwatawa, "The Prophet," younger brother of Tecumseh. An Indian Holy Man who lent spiritual fervor to Tecumseh's federation. Opposed Harrison—and lost— at Battle of Tippecanoe, 1811. 1832 portrait by George Catlin: Courtesy Tippecanoe Battlefield, Indiana

19

Tippecanoe, fought in early November 1811, was proclaimed an American victory, but it only stirred the red men to greater wrath. Within months a major war raged through the Northwest (now the upper Midwest) as tribesmen carried tomahawk and scalping knife against outlying settlements.

That backwoods skirmishing helped lead the United States into a major war. For years resentment had flamed against England's naval policies. Locked in a death struggle with France's Napoleon, Britain was attempting to starve its enemy into submission by blocking all trade with the Continent. American ship after American ship, deep-loaded with grain or tobacco or rum, was halted by English warships, its cargo confiscated, and some of its crew pressed into service in the British navy. Each capture sent a surge of indignation through the South and West where the spirit of nationalism ran high. Only a war with England would avenge the national honor, westerners believed; too, war would allow the capture of the Canadian forts where (the frontiersmen agreed) Tecumseh had been supplied by the English with arms and encouragement. In the then-Southwest, war would allow an attack on Spanish Florida, for Spain was England's ally.

Western pressure was vital in goading President James Madison to recommend war in June 1812, but western dreams of a speedy conquest of Canada soon were shattered. An invading army crossed the Detroit River with Fort Malden as its objective, but was sent scurrying as the forts at Mackinac and Dearborn fell to British and Indians who raided deep into Ohio. Not until the autumn of 1813 could the United States take the initiative. Its first step was to win control of Lake Erie; this was accomplished by a twenty-seven year old stripling, Oliver Hazard Perry, whose home-built fleet scattered the British navy in a furious three-hour engagement fought in early September 1813, at Put-in-Bay on South Bass Island. Harrison heard the good news when a messenger delivered a dispatch scrawled on the back of an old envelope: "We have met the enemy and they are ours." Acting at once, Harrison ferried his well-trained army across the lake, descended on Fort Malden and pursued its defenders eastward, then soundly defeated them at the Battle of the Thames (5 October 1813). Tecumseh and his leading chiefs were killed; some were skinned to provide razor strops for their victors. A year later a rising young frontiersman, Andrew Jackson, led a thousand yelling Tennessee militiamen into the Creek village of Tohopeka on the Horseshoe Bend of the Tallapoosa River. The Creeks fought bravely, but the bodies of eight hundred of their finest warriors littered the battlefield that night. These two decisive battles broke the spirit of the red men. Cowed and humiliated, they could be browbeaten into surrendering their tribal homelands. Once more the westward march of the pioneers began.

When the War of 1812 ended in 1815 the settled areas of the United States formed a giant triangle, its base along the Atlantic seaboard, its apex at the junction of the Ohio and Mississippi rivers. To the north lay the virgin forests of the upper Mississippi Valley —a wilderness Eden where the countryside had been flattened and enriched by the last glaciers of the Ice Age, and where the humus-rich soil was "so fat that it will grease your fingers." One traveler was told that the settlers made candles by dipping wicks in mud puddles! To the south were the fertile plains and bottom-lands of western Georgia, Alabama and Mississippi, still largely unsettled, where fortunes could be made. You could grow a glamorous new crop there, cotton, only recently made marketable by an ingenious Yankee, Eli Whitney, who invented a "gin" to clean the burr-like seeds from the fibers. Here was opportunity unlimited for the pioneers; they could convert the Mississippi Valley into the granary and clothier of the world.

The shock troops of the army of settlers who moved northward into the upper Mississipi Valley were recruited from the southern back-country, where thousands of small farmers were being dislodged by the westward advance of cotton plantations. Some followed the trails to Pittsburgh, bought or built crude flatboats, and drifted down the river to their destinations. Travelers reported a regular procession of these ungainly craft on the broad Ohio, a sweating farmer at the sweeps, the housewife busy with cooking or the wash, children running about the deck, a horse and a cow or two contentedly munching hay in the prow. Other pioneers trekked westward along the newly built National Road, a crushed-stone road financed by the federal government that led from Cumberland on the Potomac to Wheeling on the Ohio

Battle of Tippecanoe, Nov. 7,
1811. Contemporary
lithograph by P. S. Duval.
While Tecumseh was in the
South arousing resistance,
Harrison won a close victory
at Prophetstown, Tecumseh
and Tenskwatawa's home
base. Courtesy Indiana
Historical Society

Left: *"Fairview Inn,"* Thomas
Coke Ruckle. *The road west
was often a crowded one.*
Courtesy Maryland Historical
Society

"Canal Scene," Currier & Ives.
*The opening of the Erie Canal
in 1825 greatly facilitated
westward emigration. This
scene (canal boats often
traveled all night) is near
Little Falls, N.Y.* Courtesy
Canal Museum, Syracuse

by 1818, and eventually on into Illinois. "We are," wrote a traveler, "seldom out of sight, as we travel this grand track, of family groups before and after us." Most camped by the roadside at night, lighting the forest for miles on end. "Old America seems to be breaking up and moving westward," an observer noted. Indiana and Illinois followed Ohio into the Union as states in 1816 and 1818.

This was but the beginning. In the early 1830s, as the population stream from the South began to slow because of the filling of the hilly upcountry just north of the Ohio River, a new army of settlers began the assault on the level prairie country of northern Indiana and Illinois. They came from the New England hills, where sheep growing was displacing farming as the spawning textile mills of that region provided a market for wool. As the mania for sheep swept the countryside, thousands upon thousands of farmers saw their lands usurped for pasturage and were forced to leave, some to seek jobs in the mills, more to join the trek westward. The "rural decay" of New England had begun.

The route of the New Englanders westward was still along the Mohawk Valley, but now they traveled in style. The Erie Canal, between the Hudson River and Lake Erie, opened in 1825, provided an all-water route to the interior that was safe, sure, and cheap. Travel on the mule-drawn barges might be slow, the food abominable, and the mosquitoes ravenous, but the emigrant was certain to reach Buffalo, where he could buy deck passage to Detroit for only a few dollars. A thrifty pioneer, not too concerned with comfort, could travel from Massachusetts to Michigan for ten or fifteen dollars.

Such an investment was nothing compared with the profits waiting at the end of the trail, for the Erie Canal assured them a choice of markets for their cereals and livestock. They could ship either eastward over the canal to the food-hungry consumers of the Northeast, or southward on the Mississippi River to New Orleans. Just at this time the Mississippi steamboat was coming into its own; by 1825 75 navigated the river and by 1840 no less than 187. And what glamorous creations they were! Wags might describe the ungainly craft as "an engine on a raft with $11,000 worth of jigsaw work," but their high-pressure engines were so powerful and their hulls so shallow that they could navigate the smallest streams; some captains boasted that their vessels could operate on a heavy dew. Best of all, they lowered freight rates from Louisville to New Orleans from five dollars a ton in 1810 to twenty-five cents a ton in 1840. The steamboats, with the Erie Canal, allowed a choice of markets that guaranteed against hard times for all Yankees and Yorkers with gumption enough to begin life anew.

So they came, by the thousands, in a "Great Migration" that jammed the canal boats and highways. They disembarked at some terminal point, then spread over the countryside. Detroit, conveniently reached by lake steamboats, was their first mecca. Within five years after 1831 that hamlet exploded into a city of ten thousand souls, complete with a library, a museum, a public garden, and street lights of such remarkable inefficiency that (if we may believe the local editor) only a few more were needed to plunge the city into total darkness. From Detroit the settlers moved inland, along the river valleys first, then over the uplands until Michigan's statehood was possible in 1837.

By this time the emigrant stream was flowing toward Chicago. In 1836 no less than 450 vessels disgorged their human cargoes there and this was but the beginning. "Our streets are thronged with wagons loaded with household furniture and the implements necessary to farming," one editor reported. "Foot-passengers, too, with well-filled sacks on their shoulders come in large numbers." All the Northeast seemed bound for the lush farmlands that lay beyond this gate of opportunity.

The forested areas of northern Illinois filled first, for the frontiersmen were distrustful of the prairie that alternated with woodlands in the upper Mississippi Valley; in their experience the soil's fertility could be judged by the density of its timber growth. Gradually, however, bolder souls experimented with grassland farms, hugging the woodlands first, then extending over the open plains. As these succeeded, other farmers followed, pushing even onto the "Grand Prairie" of central Illinois where the flower-draped countryside stretched unbroken to the horizon. With the best lands in northern Illinois disappearing, later comers journeyed northward from Chicago, or westward from the newer embarkation point at Milwaukee, to begin the conquest of Wisconsin. Many came from New England and New York, but they were joined now by increasing numbers from Germany and Scandinavia—sturdy peasants who taught their less-thrifty Yankee neighbors how to conserve the soil, to hoard grain against a day of disaster, and to build great barns to protect their livestock from the cold. When Wisconsin became a state in 1848 one-third of its people were foreign-born.

Long before this time westerners were demanding that the lands just west of the Mississippi be opened to settlement. A needless Indian war, fought against Chief Black Hawk when his followers refused to leave their ancestorial lands in the Rock River Valley of Illinois, provided the needed excuse. In 1833 the "Black Hawk Purchase" opened much of eastern Iowa to pioneers. Other "purchases" followed, as the disheartened Indians were cajoled into ceding tract after tract. When the last tract was officially opened to settlers at midnight on 30 April 1843, thousands surrounded its borders, ready to rush pell-mell when the guarding troops fired their guns in the air. Already the "boomer" psychology was appearing among frontiersmen. The best lands of the West were running out, they feared, and those who did not grab their share now would be lost forever. When Iowa became a state in 1846 pioneers already were shouldering their way into Minnesota, although that territory did not enter the Union until 1858.

While Yankees, Yorkers, and sturdy European peasants transformed the upper Mississippi Valley into a paradise of small farms, other pioneeers in the old Southwest reared a "cotton kingdom" of giant plantations and one-horse farms—all resting on the mudsill of slavery. Their westward march began when the Battle of Horseshoe Bend broke the power of the Indians, opening the way for their removal. This came with sickening speed. Time after time in the years after 1817 government agents assembled a few corrupt chiefs, cajoled or bribed them into making their "X" on a treaty that ceded their tribe's lands to the United States, and ordered the tribe to pack up and leave in return for gifts and lands beyond the Mississippi. Protests were in vain; often they were answered by soldiers who drove the heartsick red men westward at bayonet point. By the mid-1840s the last Indians had followed their "Trail of Tears" to reservations in the Indian Territory of modern Oklahoma.

Long before the last word was written in this unsavory chapter of the history of man's treatment of man, homeseekers were flooding over the ceded lands. First came the small farmers—men of small means but large ambition—who made the first scars on the wilderness: cutting away a few trees, building a rough cabin, relying as much on the rifle as the plow to feed an ever-growing family. A year or so later an eastern planter was likely to appear, making sure the land was fertile before risking a sizeable investment in slaves. If prospects seemed good he would buy out the "improvements" of a dozen small farmers, who moved on westward to begin the process anew. The planter hurried eastward to sell his worn fields, then returned the following spring, leading a procession of wagons laden with household goods, herds of cattle and horses, and a band of slaves marching under the watchful eyes of an overseer. Once arrived, fields were cleared by the slaves, cotton planted on the rich soil, and a stately mansion constructed. If the planter had chosen well his bountiful profits allowed him to buy out other small farmers nearby, building his plantation to the thousand-acre size that had proven most efficient. This process was repeated over and over again as the cotton kingdom took shape. By the 1850s two-thirds of the nation's cotton supply was grown there.

Some planters and farmers who succeeded were content to settle down, develop their lands and "grow up with the country," in the phrase of the day. But a restless fringe would have none of that. These were the "men with the West in their eyes," congenital wanderers who would have been unhappy in Paradise. Ahead—west—was always something better. "This is a land of plenty," one told a visitor, "but we are proceeding to a land of abundance." They were off at the slightest excuse. A hint that their fields had lost their youthful fertility, rumors of rich lands ahead, neighbors pressing too closely upon them, and they were away, never contented if a white man lived between them and sundown. Travelers in Ohio, marveling at abandoned farms amidst still uncleared fields, were told that their owners had gone to Indiana; in Indiana they learned that Illinois had beckoned; in Illinois they heard that Iowa or Missouri was the new mecca. "He lives and dies in hope,"

"Trail of Tears" by Robert Lindneux. Increasing demand for Indian lands in the East led to the Indian Removal Policy of the 1830s. Many officials, including some sincerely sympathetic to the Indians' plight, felt that the only alternative to extermination was for the Indians to be removed to unclaimed lands beyond the Mississippi. The policy was carried out sporadically, but eventually failed: American expansion failed to halt at the Mississippi. Courtesy Wollaroc Museum, Bartlesville, Oklahoma

wrote one who knew the breed well, though he might have added that those hopes seldom were realized.

These were the restless nomads who were to challenge the vastness of the trans-Mississippi West. The occupation of the territories bordering the Father of Waters posed no problems; Missouri filled so rapidly that it became a state in 1821 and Arkansas followed in 1836. But beyond lay a chain of Indian reservations, granted to the transplanted eastern tribes for "so long as the trees shall grow, the waters run"; and beyond these lay the semiarid Great Plains that had been labeled the "Great American Desert" by early explorers. This vast barrier must be crossed to reach the fertile coastal valleys of California and Oregon, two thousand miles away. Here was a task to challenge the courage of the most restless pioneers.

Happily they were worthy of the challenge. Toughened by rough-and-tumble life in a raw new land where the law was carried in holsters and boot-tops, as swaggeringly proud of their country as they were disdainful of all others, these self-styled "half-horse, half-alligator, star-spangled ring-tailed roarers" were ideal colonizers. What mattered it that they were entering a land where harsh nature stood guard over its treasures, where rival colonizers already were entrenched? They were ready, even eager to trade civilization for the pot at the end of the rainbow. These were the reckless pioneers who were to shoulder their way across the continent, brush aside Indians and rival colonizers alike, and carry the boundaries of their country to the Pacific.

Names, location, and photographer unknown: These were Americans who went west. Courtesy Denver Public Library, Western History Department

Pioneers of the Far West

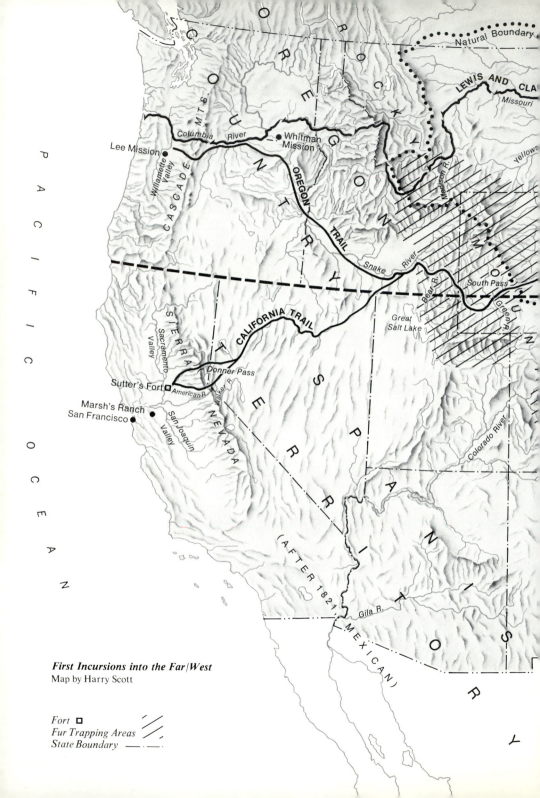

First Incursions into the Far/West
Map by Harry Scott

Fort ☐
Fur Trapping Areas
State Boundary ——

Lake Superior

Louisiana Purchase

XPEDITION

Lake Michigan

G R E A T

Chicago

L O U I S I A N A

OREGON TRAIL

Platte River

Missouri River

St. Joseph

P L A I N S

Independence

St. Louis

Pike's Peak

SANTA FE TRAIL

Arkansas R.

P U R C H A S E

Mississippi River

Santa Fe

Natural Boundary of Louisiana Purchase

Red River

T E X A S

(SPANISH; 1821, MEXICAN; 1836, INDEPENDENT)

Brazos R.

Washington

Austin

Colorado R.

San Antonio

Rio Grande

GULF OF MEXICO

| 100 | 200 | 300 Miles |
| 100 | 200 | 300 | 400 | 500 Kilometers |

The Far West was a land of vast distances and distant horizons, a land where nature had piled obstacle on obstacle to block the westward march of the pioneers. There were the gargantuan grasslands known as the Great Plains, the towering peaks of the Rockies and High Sierra perpetually clothed in snow, the barren uplands of sagebrush-covered plateaus, and the parched deserts where men and animals died like flies. Only in a few spots was sufficient water available for farming, and many of these were already occupied. The Pacific Northwest was claimed by England; all the Southwest was claimed by Spain or, after its independence in 1821, Mexico. These lands were sparsely settled; perhaps seven hundred fur traders held the Northwest for Britain, while some four thousand Mexicans lived in Texas and California, and forty thousand more in New Mexico. But all were firmly entrenched, and all fiercely determined to guard their holdings.

Americans were scarcely aware of their presence until 1803 when Thomas Jefferson's fortunate real-estate speculation added the ill-defined but immense Louisiana Territory to the United States. The exploration of this giant province by governmental expeditions showed Americans something of the importance of the Louisiana Purchase, and a bit of the problems they might face in its occupation. The most important expedition, that of Meriwether Lewis and William Clark along the Missouri-Columbia river route to the Pacific between 1803 and 1806, brought back cheering news of fur-bearing animals in the northern Rockies, but later explorations were less encouraging. Zebulon Montgomery Pike, investigating in 1806-07 the region around the peak that bears his name, fell prey to a Spanish army. They not only escorted him to a Mexican lock-up but ingloriously relieved him of all his records before dumping him back across the border. That disaster lessened enthusiasm for exploration, and another expedition in 1820 produced even more disastrous results. Major Stephen H. Long, its commander, after a vain search for the illusive head-waters of the Red River, returned with news that the whole Great Plains was a desert forever unsuitable for white occupation. That label— "Great American Desert"—spread across the maps of the day, and discouraged the occupation of the region for a generation to come.

Upper: *Zebulon Pike, explorer of the southwest, most famous for discovering the peak that bears his name; and* (Lower) *Stephen Long, whose otherwise fine map unfortunately used the term "Great American Desert" for the Great Plains, and delayed recognition of the area's value for a generation.* Both portraits by Charles Willson Peale: Courtesy Independence National Historical Park

The Far West might offer few attractions to farmers, but furs were plentiful in the beaver streams, and Indians might welcome traders. So a few adventurous souls began the invasion. Some followed the Missouri River west to the northern Rocky Mountains, and others lead pack-trains of laden mules into the Southwest. One of the latter was first to find his pot of gold. William Becknell was dangerously close to Spanish New Mexico in the spring of 1821 when he was surprised by a detachment of Mexican troops. To his happy astonishment they greeted him eagerly; Mexico was now independent of Spain, they told him, and would welcome trade with the United States. Hurrying to the New Mexican capital of Santa Fe, he disposed of his supplies at a thousand percent profit and hurried back to Missouri for more. Thus was born the Santa Fe trade. Each spring thereafter dozens of merchants and their helpers gathered at one of the Missouri River towns—Franklin or Independence or Westport. They loaded their covered wagons with knives and blankets and hardware and Yankee gimcracks, and plodded off along the nine hundred mile trail to Santa Fe, forming a procession a mile long.

A wearisome journey that was, across arid plains and deserts and mountains, but the rewards were great. All was bustle and excitement in the sleepy Mexican town as the caravan arrived. Its drivers had scrubbed and shaved and combed to attract the dark-eyed senoritas, and now they circled the plaza amidst shouts of "Los Americanos! La entrada de la caravana!" "I doubt," one trader wrote, "whether the first sight of the walls of Jerusalem were beheld by the crusaders with much more tumultous and soul-enrapturing joy." The Santa Fe trade was as rich in profits as in romance. Each year the loads of silver bullion, gold, furs, and mules that burdened the traders' returning wagons stirred the economy of the Mississippi Valley; each tale that they told of Mexico's weak hold on its northern province whetted expansionists' appetite for more land.

The first fur trappers to invade the Rocky Mountain country were less fortunate. Lured westward by the reports of Lewis and Clark that the northern Rockies were teeming with beaver, a band of Missourians formed the Missouri Fur Company in 1809. They raised a modest amount of capital and

"Fording the Cimarron" and "Traders' Wagons Arriving in Santa Fe," Nick Eggenhofer. The Santa Fe Trail was the great trade route that secured the Southwest to the United States. The Cimarron was a welcome watercourse, coming *after a hazardous "jornada," or desert crossing, about half way in the journey. Finally the great wagons, heavily loaded with American trade goods, arrived at the Mexican capital of Santa Fe. Eggenhofer is a contemporary American artist* *and life-long student of transportation in the old West.* Courtesy of the Artist

*"Whisky! Whisky!" and
"Trader at Pierre's Hole,"
John Clymer. The fur trade: a
great saga unique in American
history. Superbly skilled
mountain men spent the year
trapping in remote places,
then came roaring in to the
annual rendezvous at some
mountain "hole," or valley,
to trade the year's take for a
few supplies and a week's
debauch. These superb paintings
are accurate in both historical
detail and geography.*
Courtesy of the Artist

dispatched expeditions up the Missouri to the Yellowstone River valley, where posts were built and trade begun. This proved disastrous; the log fortifications symbolized white occupation to the Indians, and stirred a succession of attacks that cost heavily in lives and goods. They also helped create some of the first authentic heroes in the history of the Far West.

Such a man was John Colter, a compulsive wanderer, who had been with Lewis and Clark but decided to stay on in the mountains rather than return to civilization. There he entered the service of the Missouri Fur Company, and there he endured one of the harshest trials ever inflicted on a westerner. Paddling down a stream with a lone companion near the Three Forks of the Missouri, Colter blundered into a camp of several hundred Blackfoot Indians. His companion was killed, but to his surprise Colter was turned loose as the old men of the tribe motioned for him to run away. He was wise enough to know what to expect now; he was to be the prize in a "race for life" and would win his freedom if he could outdistance the young warriors. The Madison River was only five miles away; if he could reach it he might escape. By the time he was halfway there blood was gushing from his nose and mouth, and he had to rest. Pausing, he saw that one Indian was only a few yards away, with the others far back. When the warrior rushed, lance poised for the kill, Colter wrestled the weapon from him, killed him with his own lance, and ran on, with some hope now. He reached the Madison safely and hid himself so skillfully that the Indians searched for him in vain, then he started on foot to join his companions three hundred miles away. When he arrived eleven days later he was so emaciated that his friends did not recognize him. Yet he returned to his trap lines a few days later. Western heroes of that day were made of hardy stuff.

Indian attacks and the expenses of the long river journey to the Yellowstone country forced a shift in trading techniques that launched the fur trade on its golden era. Its genius was a Missourian, William Henry Ashley, who had suffered heavy losses in the northern Rockies. Hearing Indian tales of rich beaver streams just west of the central Rockies, Ashley financed a small exploring expedition under Jedediah Strong Smith. Smith was a twenty-three year old, well-educated, Bible-toting New Englander destined to become the nation's most adventurous explorer. With a few companions, Smith in 1823 crossed the central Rockies through a broad portal since known as South Pass (in present-day Wyoming), thus unwittingly blazing the trail soon to be followed by the emigrant wagon trains. Just beyond he found the Green River as overflowing with beaver as the Indians had said. Ashley, hurrying westward to the scene of his good fortune in the spring of 1825, scattered the trappers he had brought with him with instructions to meet at a designated point some weeks later. Thus was born the "rendezvous system," and with it the trade's most glamorous era.

For the next fifteen years some six hundred trappers lived continuously in the Far West, wandering always in a constant search for untrapped beaver streams. Their only contact with civilization was at the annual rendezvous. This was held at some agreed-upon spot in July, when the "mountain men" from all the West assembled to meet a caravan of merchants from St. Louis who were willing to risk the journey for profits of two thousand percent. There was trading as the "hairy bank notes" were exchanged for knives, guns, ammunition, traps, and a few luxuries that the forests could not provide. The flat casks of raw alcohol were opened, and the rendezvous was transformed into a scene of roaring debauchery. Day after day the lethal fluid was passed about as the mountain men staged horse races or brutal wrestling matches, fought duels that usually ended in the death of one participant, or gambled away their year's earnings, their horses, their Indian wives, even their own scalps. Then, men and earnings exhausted, they stumbled away into the forests to begin the fall hunt.

The day of the mountain man was short-lived, for excessive profits bred competition, and competition spelled the extermination of the beaver. For a time a combination of traders led by Jedediah Strong Smith that came to be known as the Rocky Mountain Fur Company was in control, but merchants from St. Louis and Santa Fe soon challenged their monopoly. In the early 1830s the giant American Fur Company, long dominant in the Great Lakes, entered the field. As these two giants struggled for supremacy, they encouraged such ruthless over-trapping that by the 1840s the beaver was virtually exterminated. At the

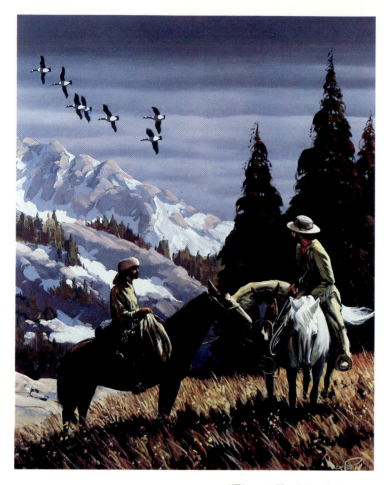

"Time to Head South,"
Roy Kerswill. By 1840 the
boom days of the fur trade
were over, but the superbly
skilled mountain men had
cracked open the West.
Courtesy Jefferson National
Expansion Memorial

same time a shift in European styles decreed that gentlemen should wear silk toppers rather than beaver hats, and thereby lessened the market for furs. The era of the mountain man was at an end.

By this time they had played their role in history. In their endless quest for virgin beaver streams they had explored every nook and cranny of the Far West. They had sent back news of lush valleys where land could be had for the taking, of beckoning farmlands, and of passes through the mountains that brought this distant bonanza-land within reach of the Mississippi Valley. Wrote an English visitor among them, George F. Ruxton: "From the Mississippi to the mouth of the Colorado of the West, from the frozen regions of the North to the Gila of Mexico, the beaver hunter has set his traps in every creek and stream. All this vast country, but for the daring and enterprise of these men, would be even now a *Terra Incognita* to geographers." They, not the official explorers, pointed the way west to the pioneers who would soon follow.

Other propagandists also played a role. California's prophets were profit-minded merchants or speculators. Some were the "hide-and-tallow" traders—Yankee ship captains who after Mexican independence regularly visited the coast to load their vessels with hides and tallow from the vast cattle ranches that thrived there. The tallow would be sold in Peru to produce candles for miners, and the hides carried to New England to supply the burgeoning shoe industry there. Others were adventurers who silver-tongued vast land grants from Mexican officials and were eager to attract purchasers: men such as John Marsh whose Mount Diablo Ranch in the lower San Joaquin Valley was to become a loadstone for emigrants, and John A. Sutter, a rotund little Swiss who mixed bluff, deceit, and ability to create a feudal barony on the banks of the Sacramento Valley's American River, complete with an adobe fort with bastions bristling with cannons and with walls eighteen feet high. Marsh and Sutter were only two of the tub-thumpers for California; their letters and reports, widely printed in the East, pictured a paradise where perpetual sunshine, soils of incredible richness, and Mexican officials too lazy to collect taxes created opportunity for the farmer unrivaled this side of Heaven.

The Oregon country's most effective propagandists were gentlemen of the cloth. Missionary concern

John Augustus Sutter, remarkable adventurer, entrepreneur, and colonizer of the Sacramento Valley, whose propaganda efforts did much to publicize California in the East. Later the discovery of gold on land he claimed made such propaganda unnecessary. Artist unknown: Courtesy California State Library

for that distant land was sparked by the appearance of four Oregon Indians in St. Louis in 1831. They had come to look and be entertained, but a writer in the Methodist *Christian Advocate and Journal,* eager to stir interest in missions, branded them the "wise men of the West" who had made their arduous journey to seek salvation through "the white man's Book of Heaven." As funds poured in the first missionaries started west, a band of Methodists under the Reverend Jason Lee. Arriving in the Oregon country in the autumn of 1834, they established their mission in the rich Willamette Valley where Indians were few but farming prospects excellent. Others followed, including the Reverend Marcus Whitman who was to gain fame and martyrdom when massacred by the Cayuse Indians in 1847. All bombarded the East with appeals for funds, or traveled widely lecturing on the beauties of Oregon and its limitless prospects for farmers. Here was another Eden, waiting only the touch of man to release its riches.

This was exciting news to Mississippi Valley farmers. They—or at least the restless fringe among them—were ready to be on the move. Good farming lands were still plentiful in the neighborhood, of course, but how could these compare to the lush fields that waited them in the far West? The propagandists played their role so effectively that the Mississippi Valley frontier spawned three migratory streams over the next years. One had Texas as its goal, another was bound for California's interior valleys, and a third sought an earthly paradise in the Oregon country. None was large—less than a thousand reached California during the first years of settlement—but all were to play a major role in history. Their venturing spirit was to expand the borders of their nation to the Pacific.

Texas felt their impact first. That sparsely settled Mexican province was opened to Americans in 1821 when Moses Austin, a Missourian who had acquired Spanish citizenship, was granted the right to plant a colony between the Colorado and Brazos rivers. Moses Austin died before he could recruit his colonists, but his son, Stephen F. Austin, met the challenge. Twenty-seven years old, slight of build with the delicate features of a scholar, an accomplished flute player, Austin seemed utterly unsuited to the role of colony planter. But he was also energetic, honest, and an able administrator who could command the respect of the rough frontiersmen he was to lead. So his colony, grouped about the town of San Felipe de Austin, grew steadily: from three hundred settlers by the end of 1823—the "Old Three Hundred" in Texas legend—to more than two thousand a year later.

Austin's success opened the gates. Mexico, eager as a new republic to strengthen its northern provinces, decided in 1824 to grant vast tracts of land to promoters—the *empresarios* in the language of the day— who would guarantee to settle a hundred or more families on their holdings. Within months all Texas was divided into a crazy-quilt patchwork of grants, each controlled by a speculator who knew that he must lure a specified number of settlers in order to make good his claim. Their advertising blanketed the then-southwestern United States, promising lands of impossible cheapness, the richest soils, and the most equitable climate in all the world. Many were unable to resist; "Gone to Texas" signs appeared on abandoned cabins by the hundreds, and no less than nine thousand Americans crowded into Texas in the next five years.

Here were all the ingredients of revolution. The new settlers, blatantly proud of their homeland and openly contemptuous of their new rulers, were unable or unwilling to adjust to the religious, legal, and political institutions of Mexico. What sort of a nation was it that demanded they forsake Protestantism for Catholicism? What sort of law was it that held a man guilty until he was proven innocent? What sort of a government would deny Texans their own statehood, and insist on regulating their local affairs from distant Mexico City? A new Mexican president, General Antonio Lopez de Santa Anna, proclaimed himself a permanent dictator, dismissed congress, and abolished the federal system in favor of centralized control. The Texas-Americans (who outnumbered the Texan-Mexicans by three-to-one) could take no more. Meeting at San Felipe de Austin in November 1835, they formed a provisional government dedicated not to independence, but to a return to the federal principles traditional in Mexico.

Santa Anna would have none of that. With a rag-tag army of nearly six thousand men and hangers-on he started northward. As he entered Texas his way was blocked by a little band of 187 patriots who had barricaded themselves in an abandoned mission in San Antonio, the Alamo. They were few, but their leaders were of a sort to inspire awe—Davy Crockett and Jim Bowie and Buck Travis—and all were pledged to "liberty or death." For ten days the *diablos Tejanos* fought off assault after assault, only to be overwhelmed on 6 March 1836. All paid for their bravery with their lives, but nearly sixteen hundred Mexican dead were counted on the battlefield, and "Remember the Alamo" became a slogan that united Texas.

This unity was needed, for independence had already been declared. Meeting in a drafty shed where the chill blasts of a "norther" sent the thermometer tumbling to the freezing mark, fifty-nine delegates had gathered in the village of Washington, Texas, to declare their freedom from Mexico on 2 March 1836. They had adopted a constitution and named a famed Indian fighter, Sam Houston, commander of their army. Houston had taken some time to whip his raw troops into shape, and now he was retreating eastward with Santa Anna's soldiers on his heels. He made his stand on the banks of the San Jacinto River in east Texas on 21 April. Shouting "Remember the Alamo," the Texans charged the enemy lines just as the Mexicans were settling down for their usual siesta. Within moments the Battle of San Jacinto was over with 630 of the enemy dead and 730 more, including General Santa Anna, prisoners. This ended the fighting and launched the Republic of Texas on its ten-year period of independence.

While Texans were wresting their nation from Mexico—and laying the basis for its future annexation by the United States—other Mississippi Valley pioneers were casting covetous glances at California and Oregon. A disastrous financial panic that began in 1837 and persisted until the 1840s underlay their eagerness. Why stay at home when wheat sold for ten cents a bushel, corn rotted in the field, and steamboats burned bacon as cheaper than wood or coal? Why stagger along for years under the debt-load that individuals had assumed when they mortgaged their farms during the booming 1830s? Why endure skyrocketing taxes when 640 acres of free land waited all comers in the Sacramento Valley of California or the Willamette Valley of Oregon? These were the questions that farmers asked themselves as they heard

Upper: *"The Jumping-Off Spot,"* William H. Jackson. The steamboat part of their journey over, emigrants hastily reorganized for the long overland trek. Courtesy Scotts Bluff National Monument

Lower: *Wagon Interior.* A fascinating photograph, probably taken at journey's beginning, yet already the canvas has been patched. Wagons were filled with cargo, and only the sick actually rode. The clock (behind lamp) and the silverware certainly will be discarded as draft animals give out, possibly also the chair, bedstead, and family Bible. Probably a cow along: note butter churn beyond bed. The accordion (above bedstead) and banjo (exteme left) will sound by campfires on summer nights. The spinning wheel, light and useful, may be in Oregon today. Courtesy University of Illinois Press

propagandists preach of the opportunities waiting the ambitious in the Eldorados hidden beyond the western horizon. As "California Fever" and "Oregon Fever" raged across the Mississippi Valley, hundreds of the venturesome sold their worn fields for a pittance, converted their farm wagons into prairie schooners, and turned their steps toward Independence, Missouri, the jumping-off spot for the California and Oregon trails.

The first sizeable band to make the journey gathered there in the spring of 1841—a pitiful little group of sixty-nine persons with total cash assets of less than a hundred dollars, no knowledge of overland travel, and only the faintest notion of where they were bound. "We knew only that California lay to the

West," wrote their leader, John Bidwell. So westward they marched, out along the Platte River, upward through South Pass, and into the Bear River Valley of Utah. There they divided, some to follow the Oregon Trail along the Snake and Columbia rivers to Jason Lee's mission in the Willamette Valley, and the remainder—thirty-two men, one woman, and one child—to follow Bidwell across the burning sands of Nevada until the towering Sierra blocked their path. Climbing first along the swift-flowing Walker River, then wandering blindly amidst the maze of peaks and valleys, they finally emerged at John Marsh's ranch in the San Joaquin Valley with enough spirit left to criticize the sun-withered fields and crumbling adobe dwellings of their host.

Others crowded on their heels. The 1842 migration was insignificant, but the next year a thousand persons and eighteen hundred cattle waited at Independence for the grass to green. A major emigration such as this required organization. Pausing before they entered the Indian country the pioneers adopted a high-flown constitution "for the purpose of keeping good order and promoting civil and military discipline," listened to a deluge of spread-eagle oratory from candidates, and prepared to elect a "Council of Ten" that would exercise legislative and judicial functions on the trail. Voting booths were absent on that prairie land, hence frontier ingenuity was called into play. Each candidate scampered away from the crowd, with his followers falling in behind him to be counted. This, a visiting journalist noted, was literally "running for office."

The most difficult problem faced by the Council of Ten had to be solved only a few days later; those without cattle complained that those with cattle were slowing the march. Let the party divide, the Council decided, those without livestock moving ahead, and a "cow column" following more slowly. Thus began a routine that became second nature to men and animals alike. Each day began at daybreak when shouts from the night-guards stirred sleepy-eyed wives into building a buffalo-chip fire and preparing breakfast, while their husbands harnessed the draft animals. Then tents were struck and the creaking wagons fell into position, stretching across the plains in a mile-long column. A "pilot" ranged ahead to mark stream crossings and camp sites. Wagoners walked beside their teams flicking their long whips; wives and children scattered to romp or pick wild flowers. A pause for "nooning" and a light lunch, and the column was under way again, with women napping in the wagons and the men nodding as they trudged beside their teams. At nightfall the wagons were drawn into a great circle, animals let out to graze under the night guards, fresh bread baked to go with the fat salt pork or occasional buffalo hump ribs, stories told about the campfires, or a fiddler pressed into service for an impromptu square dance. Gradually drowsiness hurried the emigrants into their blankets, for insomnia was unknown in that invigorating air. Thus the march went on, day after day, with ten, fifteen, even twenty miles covered, and with only an occasional lay-over to allow housewives to catch up on their washing.

"Hitching Up." William H. Jackson sketched the morning's most trying chore—a chore he did often. Courtesy Scotts Bluff National Monument

The 1843 caravan demonstrated that large parties were unsuited to overland travel; conflicts were frequent as tempers wore thin, and grass scarce as draft animals over-cropped the prairies. That lesson learned, travel over the next years was largely in smaller parties. Five parties reached California in 1844 and three reached Oregon, and a year later the numbers were the same. In 1846 the figures were reversed, with thirteen hundred fifty emigrants reaching the Oregon Country, and only about three hundred arriving in the Sacramento Valley. Among the California-bound were those of the ill-fated Donner Party. Starting late, and then blundering into an untested route that cost them more time, the eighty-nine pioneers recruited by Jacob and George Donner of Illinois were trapped in the High Sierra by an early snowstorm. Only forty-five were alive when rescue parties reached them that spring, and these only because they had resorted to cannibalism, subsisting on the bodies of their dead comrades. Mother nature could be a harsh task-master in the Far West.

By the mid-1840s some six thousand Americans lived in the Willamette Valley of Oregon and nearly one thousand in California, most of these clustered about Sutter's Fort in the Sacramento Valley. Here was a potentially explosive grouping. The Americans had left the United States physically but not emotionally; in their own eyes they were Americans still, and confidently believed that they were not expatriots but advance agents of an expanding republic. More-

William H. Jackson went west in 1866 as a bull-whacker on the Oregon Trail, sketchbook in hand. He is best known for the pioneering photography he did later, yet his watercolors remian valuable historical documents. All courtesy Scotts Bluff National Monument

Upper: *"Approaching Chimney Rock,"* one of the landmarks of the trail. Note that separate wagon trains often camped within sight of one another.

Center: *"Three Island Crossing,"* a dangerous fording of the Snake River.

Lower: *"Barlow Cut-Off,"* a way cut through the forest around Mount Hood. It was difficult, but avoided the dangerous rapids and high raft fees on the Columbia.

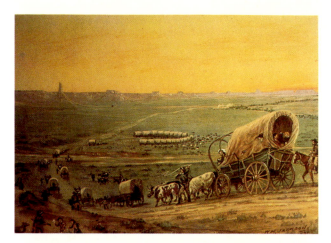

over, they were contemptuously disdainful of their new rulers: the Mexicans who owned California, and the British Hudson's Bay Company, a giant fur-trading empire that actually controlled most of the Oregon country. The stage was set for a series of international confrontations that would end with the flag of the United States planted firmly on the shores of the Pacific.

"Prairie Sun," W. H. D. Koerner. Courtesy Ruth Koerner Oliver

Settlement Flows Westward

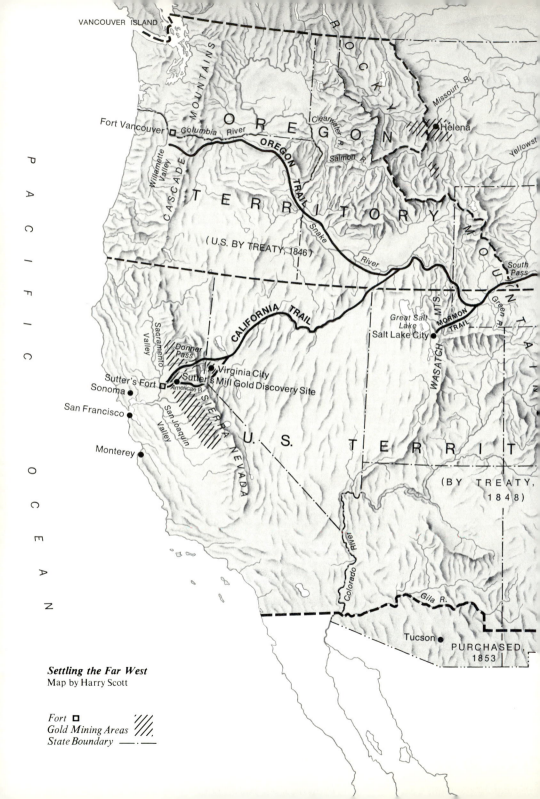

VANCOUVER ISLAND

P A C I F I C

O C E A N

ROCKY

Missouri R.

Helena

Yellowst.

Fort Vancouver
Columbia   River

Clearwater R.

OREGON

Salmon R.

CASCADE MOUNTAINS

Willamette Valley

T E R R I T O R Y

OREGON TRAIL

(U.S. BY TREATY, 1846)

Snake

River

MOUNTAIN

South
Pass

Green R.

Sacramento
Valley

Donner
Pass

CALIFORNIA   TRAIL

Great Salt
Lake

Salt Lake City

WASATCH MTS.

MORMON TRAIL

Sutter's Fort
Sonoma

Virginia City
American R.
Sutter's Mill Gold Discovery Site

San Francisco

San Joaquin
Valley

SIERRA NEVADA

U. S.   T E R R I T

San Francisco

Monterey

(B Y   T R E A T Y,
1 8 4 8)

Colorado   River

Gila R.

Tucson

PURCHASED,
1853

Settling the Far West
Map by Harry Scott

Fort ☐
Gold Mining Areas ///
State Boundary —·—

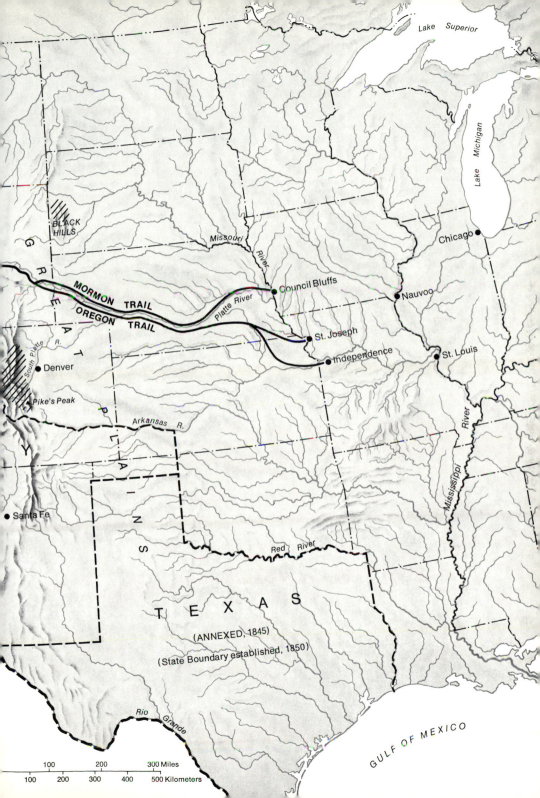

The term "manifest destiny" did not enter the nation's vocabulary until 1845, but long before this the American people were convinced that their God-given duty was to extend their country's benevolent rule over Texas and California and Oregon and all the Far West. Surely a kindly Deity did not intend their perfect democratic institutions to be narrowly confined! The ignorant peons of Mexico must be liberated, the despot-ridden British of the Oregon country freed from autocratic rule. "Prophecy," wrote one exuberant expansionist, "looks forward to the time when the valley of the Mississippi shall overflow with a restless population, and Europe be subjected to a new migration." Even war was justified to fulfill this divine purpose. Americans showed they were willing to risk war in 1844 when they chose James K. Polk as their president on a Democratic platform calling for the "re-occupation of Oregon and the re-annexation of Texas." The United States was committed to a Pacific boundary, whatever the consequences.

Texas fell first. That the Texans and the leaders of their republic openly sought annexation was certain; less certain was the desire of the American government to annex. Northerners feared that the giant province would be split into a number of slave states. Internationalists were afraid that British manufacturers would goad their country into war to preserve Texas as a duty-free source for cotton. Their apprehensions seemed to be realized when England in 1844 proposed that France, Mexico and Texas join her in a four-power treaty guaranteeing the territorial integrity of all its signers. That treaty was never signed, but it sent a current of alarmed resentment through the United States. As the people bristled with indignation over this meddling in what they considered their own affairs, sentiment swung strongly toward annexation. Polk was yet to take office, but the retiring president, John Tyler, decided to grab the honor of adding Texas to the Union for himself. On 1 March 1845, three days before he left office, Tyler signed a joint resolution of annexation admitting Texas to the Union.

The "re-occupation of Oregon" posed more problems. That sprawling territory was shared by England and the United States under a Treaty of Joint Occupation signed in 1818 and renewed in 1827. The English government believed that the region south of the Columbia River would be awarded the United States in the eventual settlement, and that the area north of the forty-ninth parallel would remain her own. Hence she concentrated her efforts on the triangle between the river and the forty-ninth parallel, the region actually in dispute. There her powerful agent, the Hudson's Bay Company, built Fort Vancouver on the north bank of the Columbia as its headquarters, and established traders and nearly a thousand farmers there as permanent residents. The American pioneers, on the other hand, were concentrated in the Willamette Valley south of the area in dispute. This was the situation when President Polk, riding on the crest of public sentiment for "All Oregon or None," in December 1845 ended joint occupation and demanded a settlement with Britain. If possession were nine points of the law he would have to resort to war to oust the British from the disputed territory.

War seemed near as both nations flexed their military muscles, but then—suddenly and amazingly —the situation changed. The Hudson's Bay Company announced that it was shifting its headquarters from Fort Vancouver in the area under dispute to Fort Victoria on distant Vancouver Island, thus signaling that it was willing to abandon the lands north of the Columbia. The six thousand American frontiersmen living in the Willamette Valley were responsible for this amazing move. To a man they hated the Hudson's Bay Company for standing between them and the protection of the United States. What would prevent them from storming across the Columbia River some night and burning that tinder-dry structure, Fort Vancouver, to the ground? Why risk the £100,000 worth of goods and furs stored there? Better to give up a few square miles of wilderness than lose those valuables. With the way to a settlement cleared by the Company's move, England's ministers informed President Polk that they would settle on the forty-ninth parallel boundary. On 10 June 1846 the Oregon Treaty was signed, adding another princely domain to the expanding West.

Nor was this the end. California had long been ripe for the plucking. Since Mexico had won its independence in 1821, revolutions and counter-revolutions had kept the remote province in chaos, to the disgust of the wealthier Mexican-American

"Fremont at Monterey,"
W. H. D. Koerner. John C.
Fremont and his crew of
soldier/mapmakers were
ostensibly exploring routes to
California when they became
embroiled in the revolt of
Californians from Mexico, and
the U.S. acquisition of the
territory. His role, hero or
truant, is still hotly debated.
But the state's loveliness,
shown in Koerner's painting,
beguilded him, and he returned
and served as senator.
Courtesy Ruth Koerner Oliver

ranchers and merchants. Better to cast their lot with the United States, they believed, than risk lives and property under Mexico's turbulent rule. President Polk encouraged these separatist views. Acting under instructions, the American consul at Monterey, Thomas O. Larkin, carefully built a secret pro-annexation party with the aid of a wealthy Californian, Mariano G. Vallejo, whose princely estates were centered in the village of Sonoma. If left to themselves, the ruling Mexican-American faction would almost certainly have delivered California to the United States.

Fate, however, played a different tune. Lounging about Sutter's Fort were a few-score rough-hewn frontiersmen who had little better to do than trade rumors of Mexican treachery and incompetence. With the arrival nearby of the American explorer, John C. Frémont, and a band of sixty ferociously bearded mountain men, they decided to strike. At Sonoma, they had heard, a Mexican army was forming to drive them from California. This was enough. Led by a tobacco-chewing illiterate, Ezekiel Merritt, thirty-three of the most reckless set out on an all-night ride to Sonoma where they ousted Mariano Vallejo from his bed with a demand that he surrender the province to them. Vallejo disrupted their plans for a time by serving them breakfast liberally accompanied by brandy, but after the first negotiators had succumbed to his hospitality, a teetotaling idealist, William B. Ide, took over. Articles of capitulation were signed, the Republic of California proclaimed, and a flag bearing the image of a grizzly bear raised over the Sonoma plaza. The "Bear Flag Revolt" was over, and the war for California's independence begun.

The "Bear Flag Revolt" was the home-grown variety: even its flag was jury-rigged from an unbleached cotton sheet and some paint. Whatever results it might have had were submerged in the War with Mexico. Courtesy Society of California Pioneers

Unwittingly, the Bear-Flaggers had become minor pawns in a major conflict. For years bad relations had been building between Mexico and the United States; Mexicans were convinced by events in Texas and California that their powerful northern neighbor was bent on dismembering their republic piece by piece; the United States was disgruntled by Mexico's failure to protect the lives and property of American nationals in the periodic revolutions. In this tinder-box atmosphere, Polk took advantage of a boundary dispute between Texas and Mexico to send troops to the Rio Grande country. When they were fired upon by a Mexican force he had the excuse he needed. "After repeated menaces," he told Congress, "Mexico has passed the boundary of the United States, has invaded our territory and shed American blood upon the American soil.... War exists, and, notwithstanding all our efforts to avoid it, exists by act of Mexico itself." Two days later, on 12 May 1846, war was declared.

The conflict that followed was brief, and from the American point of view, highly satisfactory. The United States wanted the Southwest and took it at once. During the early months of fighting the Army of the West under General Stephen W. Kearny occupied New Mexico without firing a shot, while a force of Bear-Flaggers and sailors from the Pacific fleet subdued California. There remained only the task of convincing Mexico that it was beaten. This was entrusted to General Winfield Scott whose army stormed ashore at Vera Cruz, blustered its way to Mexico City, and in September 1847 overran heavily fortified Chapultepec Hill which guarded the main causeway into the lake-enclosed city. In the Treaty of Guadalupe-Hidalgo, ratified by the Senate on 10 March 1848, Mexico ceded to the United States California and all the Southwest north of the Gila River. Americans had followed their Manifest Destiny to the Pacific.

Yet the first occupants of the newly won lands were not eager seekers after wealth, but rather devout members of a persecuted religious sect in quest of isolation from the cruelty of their fellow men. The Church of Jesus Christ of Latter-day Saints, or the Mormon Church as it was popularly called, had suffered the wrath of popular opinion ever since its founding in 1830 by its prophet, Joseph Smith. Harried from place to place, stoned by mobs, threatened by state officials, their prophet martyred in defense of his cause, the Mormons were finally convinced that they could find peace only on the distant frontiers. With their newly chosen leader, Brigham Young, in command they gathered at Council Bluffs near modern Omaha where they spent a miserable winter as they prepared for their epic journey. Early in the spring of 1847 a "Pioneer Band" of 143 Saints started westward, following a new "Mormon Trail" along the north bank of the Platte River to avoid the hostile Americans on its south shore. Beyond South Pass the

Nauvoo, Illinois. The homes and the temple the Mormons had to leave, to start their trek to the West. Courtesy Church Archives, Church of Jesus Christ of Latter-Day Saints

Mormons turned southward, crossed the Wasatch Mountains, and emerged on the shores of the Great Salt Lake. Here, Brigham Young decided, they would rear their Desert Zion.

There was little to gladden their hearts—only a barren plain "blistering in the burning rays of the midsummer sun . . . a seemingly interminable waste of sagebrush . . . the paradise of the lizard, the cricket and the rattlesnake." But little matter. Sustained by a supreme faith that Young's leadership was divinely inspired, the Mormons flooded their fields with water from streams that gushed from the mountains rimming their valley, planted a crop of potatoes, and began planning the spacious city where they would live. Green fields welcomed the large caravans that followed the Pioneer Band westward; by the fall of that first year some eighteen hundred Saints lived on the shores of the Great Salt Lake.

Their faith in Brigham Young's leadership was justified, for in all the history of the American frontier there was no better-ordered community than that of the Mormons. Young was wise enough to realize that their shared faith would sustain the cooperative effort needed to conquer the hostile environment. Hence individual acquisitiveness was outlawed; land was allotted according to each settler's needs, water usage controlled to the last precious drop, and social activities regulated with the group interest uppermost. The combination of an unusually harsh environment and a religious dedication that transcended individual ambition created a unique and highly successful frontier community.

Its efficiency was nowhere better exhibited than in its colonizing activities. As newcomers poured in from the East or from Europe they were organized into pioneering parties properly balanced between seasoned oldtimers and new arrivals, tradesmen and farmers, craftsmen and artisans, business and professional men. Each group was sent to a site that had already been explored, with instructions on settlement-planting and advice on the form of economic enterprise to be developed. So effective was this system that settlements spread over modern Utah and along a "Mormon Corridor" that extended into southern California. Brigham Young's dream of forming a separate "State of Deseret" from this wilderness empire faded when Congress created the

The migration of the Mormons from Illinois to the Great Salt Lake Valley is strong in Mormon memory. In 1850 Danish artist C. C. A. Christensen became a convert; his subsequent zeal can be measured by the fact that after immigrating to the U.S., he walked to Utah, pulling his belongings in a handcart. Many years later he painted 22 large scenes of Mormon history on heavy linen which rolled up like a scroll, and traveled in his wagon through the Utah country, keeping fresh the memory of the Mormon hegira.

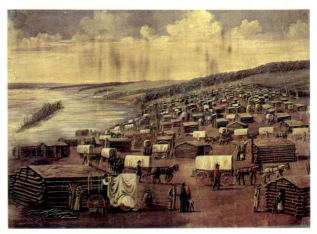

Clockwise from top right:
*"Crossing the Ice." The trek
began with the forced
evacuation of Nauvoo in the
dead of winter; indeed, the
bitter cold had frozen the
Mississippi.*

*"Winter Quarters." When they
reached the Missouri near
present-day Council Bluffs
they established a semi-
permanent camp while
preparing for the push west.
Some 600 Mormons (out of
about 12,000) died here.*

*"On the Trail." This painting
is of an earlier Mormon
journey, but shows the
wagons strung out for the
trail.*

*"Descent to Zion." After a
grueling trek that for some
had taken two years, the
wagons emerged into Great
Salt Lake Valley. Brigham
Young saw that here was both
isolation and fertility, and
the journey was over. That
afternoon they began plowing.*
Courtesy Brigham Young
University

65

Territory of Utah in 1850, but Mormon control continued there throughout the pioneer period.

Another blow to the Mormons' hope for isolation was dealt by events in California. There workmen digging a new millrace on the American River for John A. Sutter noticed flecks of yellow metal in their shovels. Much to Sutter's disgust it proved to be gold; any mining rush, he knew, would interfere with his own profitable enterprises. As well keep the Second Coming secret as a gold discovery such as this! The discovery was made on 24 January 1848; a few diggers drifted in over the next months, but not until May did the mania begin. Then, suddenly, all California went mad as carpenters dropped their hammers, farmers their plow-handles, and preachers their Bibles, to rush to the "diggings." The infection reached the East much later. On 5 December President Polk devoted a portion of his annual message to Congress to the American River's riches. "The accounts of the abundance of gold in that territory," he reported, "would scarcely command belief were they not corroborated by the authentic reports of officers in the public service." That word from on high was enough. All the nation, and much of the world, succumbed to the gold fever. The Eldorado of the old Spaniards had been found; the world was on the brink of an age of gold. Reason vanished as would-be miners fought for places on ships bound for the gold fields or prepared to start westward, singing,

O Susannah, don't you cry for me,
I'm gone to California with my wash-bowl on my knee.

Upper: *"Oh Boys I've Struck It Heavy!" by Victor Seamon. The exuberance, rarely fulfilled, that fueled the Gold Rush.* Courtesy Bancroft Library, University of California

Lower: *Abandoned ships in San Francisco Harbor. Officers and crews alike have deserted for the gold fields.* Courtesy Smithsonian Institution

The trails westward were jammed that spring of 1849: men on horses, men in buggies, men in wagons, men on foot, in such numbers that one wagon-train was seldom out of sight of those before or behind, and Indians talked seriously of moving eastward where the land surely was deserted. In all some eighty thousand Forty-Niners reached California that year, twenty-five thousand of them by sea, fifty-five thousand overland. They were well tested, for the incredible hardships of the journey took a frightening toll among the untried and inexperienced. Thousands died along the way, of the cholera that followed the wagons westward as far as the high country, of gunshot wounds, of starvation and fatigue.

*Sutter's Mill. Colonizer
John A. Sutter had this mill
built on the American River
to supply lumber for
development he hoped for
(* *see p. 45**). Workmen
deepening the millrace
discovered gold in the gravel
— and the Gold Rush was
on. Ironically Sutter was
ruined in the chaos. He died,
poor, in Washington D.C.,
unsuccessfully seeking
compensation from the
government.* Courtesy
Bancroft Library, University
of California

1

4

*J. Goldsborough Bruff, 1804-
1889: sometime sailor, West
Point student, draftsman,
gold miner—one of the chips
that floated on the great
westward tide. Bruff was
elected captain of his wagon
train that crossed in '49, and
kept an extensive journal
decorated with delightful
drawings. Later Bruff
returned to Washington,
D.C., and worked many years
in the Treasury Department.*

2

3

5

6

1. *Ferrying the Platte. Most crossings had operating ferries —for a price. The letters on the wagon stand for "Washington City and California Mining Association," which this group called itself.*

2. *Bruff called this drawing "Presence of mind-preventing a horn too much." Buffalo were a continual excitement to the pioneers, a bountiful larder, and sometimes a danger.*

3. *During the "nooning" on July 26 Bruff climbed Independence Rock to sketch the valley of the Sweetwater. He also added his name to the hundreds already carved into the rock.*

4. *"Preparing a meal." The fuel is "buffalo chips," a common substitute on the treeless plains.*

5. *Fort Laramie, where messages could be left, equipment repaired, and rumors evaluated. A welcome spot.*

6. *Accommodations in the gold fields, perhaps better than most. Shortly after this was drawn Bruff and his companions were snowed in. Courtesy Huntington Library, San Marino, California*

Upper: *The sluice box was a step beyond the prospector's pan. Water washed the gravel away, the heavier gold ores collecting on the ribbed bottom.* Courtesy Jefferson National Expansion Memorial

Lower: *Creede, Colorado. Gold often was in spectacular places, and wherever it was found, boom towns sprang up. Note construction materials piled about.* Courtesy State Historical Society of Colorado

The difficulties of the trip were as nothing compared with the suffering and disappointments that awaited them at the mines. All prospective placer sites had been appropriated by seasoned prospectors before the newcomers arrived, leaving them only abandoned mines or marginal fields. In these they labored for long hours, standing knee deep in icy streams shoveling dirt into cradles or sluice boxes where water could wash away the gravel, leaving the heavier gold behind, and at nightfall harvesting a few pennies-worth of the precious metal. Diary after diary tells the same story: wild hope, hard work, gradual disillusionment, and the final realization that they had been "humbugged."

Most soon turned to farming or merchandising, but an unhappy few were so smitten by the gold fever that they could never give up their endless quest for the "strike" of their dreams. Some of these stayed on to take jobs with the corporations that sank shafts to the veins of precious metals hidden deep in the earth, built rock-crushing mills, and accumulated the capital that signaled the coming of California's industrial age. Others fanned out over the entire West, usually in small parties with a few mules carrying all their worldly possessions. Most wandered away their lives without finding enough gold to renew their "grubstakes," but a fortunate few stumbled on fabulous deposits. Each of these "strikes" touched off a mining rush that produced a rough-and-tumble mining camp and, if the deposits proved enduring, a permanent population. These camps spread over the West between 1858 and 1876—along the Clearwater and Salmon rivers of Idaho, about Virginia City and Helena in Montana, amidst Arizona's barren mountains where such Gomorrahs as Gila City and Tucson enjoyed brief notoriety, and in the Black Hills of Dakota.

The richest of these strikes were made in Nevada and Colorado. Nevada's golden age dawned in 1859 when prospectors testing the unlikely looking soils on a peak in the Washoe Mountains (a spur jutting eastward from the Sierra) uncovered deposits of decomposed quartz rich in both gold and silver. Henry T. P. Comstock happened along just then—a drifter known as "Old Pancake" because he was too lazy to bake bread, but a good judge of pay dirt—and talked his way into a share of the claim. The discovery of the "Comstock Lode" touched off one of the West's most fantastic rushes. The thousands of prospectors, merchants, and ne'er-do-wells who flocked into the ramshackle town of Virginia City had nothing to do; every site along the Comstock Lode had already been claimed by canny San Francisco businessmen. So they spent their days marking out imaginary "mines" wherever they could find a quartz outcropping, and their nights trying to persuade the grocer to trade some beans and bacon for a few "feet" in a lode guaranteed to pay millions. Gradually, however, order replaced confusion as quartz-crushing machinery was brought in, shafts sunks to the lode, and mining begun. By 1863 Virginia City boasted a population of fifteen thousand, ornate hotels, an infinity of posh saloons, three theaters and an opera house. A year later Nevada became a state in time to cast its vote for Abraham Lincoln in the 1864 election.

The rush to the Pike's Peak country of Colorado was just as spectacular. Modest quantities of pay dirt were found on Cherry Creek and the upper South Platte River in 1858, but the "diggings" soon "played out," and the prospectors turned to town-planting instead, spending the winter laying out the community soon to be named Denver. Theirs was a smart move, for events in the Mississippi Valley that year indicated that a major rush was taking shape. A depression that slowed business in the valley to a standstill was responsible. The jobless were always fair game for promoters, particularly if they had money enough to buy shovels and washing-pans and "outfits." So the rumors spread, nurtured by editors seeking advertising and merchants wanting customers: a miner had appeared at Leavenworth with $6,000 worth of nuggets; a small boy had dug $1,000 worth of dust "and says he can get all he wants"; prospectors reported countrysides of pay dirt so rich that "gold is to be found anywhere you stick your shovel." As newspapers trumpeted this new Eldorado a hundred thousand would-be miners impatiently waited the coming of spring.

The "Rush of the Fifty-Niners" was one of the major tragi-comic events in western history. About half of the misled and ill-prepared rushers turned back before they reached Colorado; most of those who made it took one look at the pitifully small yields of the few placers in operation and turned tail for

Virginia City, Nevada. Drawing by William H. Jackson. "Ornate hotels, an infinity of posh saloons, three theaters and an opera house" in a town three years old! Courtesy Scotts Bluff National Monument

Above: *"A Forty-niner Going
Prospecting,"* *painted by*
Henry Walton from a
lithograph by Charles Nahl.
In the 1850s such one-man,
self-contained prospecting and
mining operations were
scattered through the West,
each seeking sudden wealth.
One of the few who actually
found it was John Gregory
(Opposite), *one of the first to*
strike it rich in Colorado.
Above: Courtesy Dr. A.
Shumate. Opposite: Courtesy
Colorado Historical Society

home. A few seasoned prospectors stayed on, however, for the similarities between the Rockies and California's Mother Lode country convinced them that gold was there. They were to be richly rewarded. The first major strike was made by John H. Gregory, a full-whiskered old-timer whose uncombed red hair and ragged clothes concealed his skills as a miner. In May 1859 he uncovered a quartz vein in Clear Creek that yielded four dollars worth of dust and nuggets to the pan—a rich find indeed. "Gregory Diggings" soon was bustling with activity; more important was the realization that gold was concealed in the Colorado mountains, simply awaiting finders. As prospectors combed the countryside they made strike after strike—at Tarryall and Fairplay creeks, in Boulder Canyon, on Blue Creek on the western slope—each touching off a wild rush. Colorado was on its way to a permanent population now. It became a territory in 1861 with some of its richest mineral deposits still undiscovered.

The helter-skelter scattering of mining camps over thousands and thousands of miles of western countryside brought the nation face-to-face with a troublesome problem. How could they be supplied with goods and mail? How could heavily populated California be kept in touch with the East? A few malcontents already were grumbling about their isolation and talking of a new republic. Freight could reach the West on ships making their slow way around the Horn, or on the great ox-drawn wagons of such freighting firms as Russell, Majors and Waddell, but something far speedier must be provided for letters and newspapers. Clearly private enterprise could never shoulder the expenses; only a government subsidy would do.

Congress finally awakened to its responsibility in 1857 when it promised $600,000 a year to any stagecoach company that would guarantee semiweekly service between the Mississippi Valley and California in twenty-five days or less. Here was a plum worth grabbing. The successful bidders were a little band of seasoned stagecoach operators headed by John Butterfield, and organized as the Butterfield Overland Express. They set to work with a will, laying out a 2,812-mile-long route from the western terminus of the railroad at Tipton, Missouri, to San Francisco, complete with 200 way-stations where relays of horses

Above: *A stage station in the Wyoming Territory. Brief stops at primitive accommodations were slight relief from the discomfort of the bouncing stage.* Courtesy Colorado Historical Society

Right: *An 1899 stage "outing" to the "Great Hot Springs of Dakota," which is now Hot Springs, S.D., and still a resort; only the transportation has changed. Even cross-country stagecoaches often were crowded with as many as eighteen passengers.* Courtesy South Dakota State Historical Society

could be changed and passengers fed. They purchased 1800 horses and mules, bought "celerity wagons" (light vehicles built low to the ground to prevent upsets) to be used on the unsettled portions of the route, and the lavish "Concord Coaches" that would impress travelers in populous areas, and hired the armies of drivers, hostlers, station-agents, and assorted hangers-on needed for such a gigantic operation. On Sunday, 10 October 1858, just at daybreak, the first coach swept into San Francisco, after twenty-three days and twenty-three hours on the road. "Had I not just come over the route," wrote a journalist feelingly, "I would be perfectly willing to go back on it."

He was right, for the Butterfield Overland was not for the weak or the timid. Each trip began when the passengers who had paid $200 each jammed themselves in—nine on the inside, nine more clinging to the roof—and waited for the lordly driver to mount his seat, disdainfully accept the "ribbons" from a hostler, and shout "Turn 'em loose." Away went the coach at a full gallop, enveloped in a cloud of dust, its iron wheels clattering over rocks, the passenger compartment rocking wildly on the leather thorough-braces as passengers bounced about from walls to ceiling. "We would," one wrote, "solemnly rise from our seats, bump our heads against the low roof, and, returning, vigorously ram the again-rising seat we had so incontinently left." This torture was relieved only when the coach stopped at a "station"—a filthy log or adobe hut with a mud floor, grease-encrusted stove, and furniture assembled from abandoned packing boxes. Usually it was presided over by a bearded brigand of such terrifying appearance that his guests dared not complain about the meals of fat pork, leaden bread, mesquite beans, and a lye-like fluid that passed for coffee. Sheer exhaustion after two or three days of travel allowed some passengers to doze, but others reportedly were driven insane by the ordeal.

Westerners were accustomed to so few comforts in those days that they accepted this treatment without complaint, but they did grumble their dissatisfaction over the roundabout "ox-bow route" followed by the Butterfield Express. A shorter "central route" through South Pass, they insisted, would lessen the time and expense of the journey, and would be passable in winter if the company took proper precautions. This dissatisfaction spelled opportunity for the

In their day stagecoaches were considered modern and efficient in spite of discomforts. This detail is from a stagecoach at the Museum of Westward Expansion beneath Gateway Arch, St. Louis. Photo by Joseph Matthews: Courtesy Jefferson National Expansion Memorial

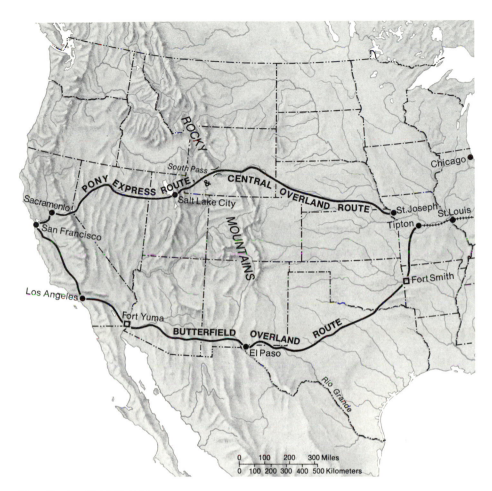

Stage Routes, Pony Express
Map by Harry Scott

giant freighting firm of Russell, Majors and Waddell. If it could use its profits to demonstrate the superiority of the South Pass route it might convince the government to transfer its subsidy northward. That was the hope when the Central Overland, California & Pike's Peak Express was formed in 1859. From the start the Central Overland was a financial disaster, losing money so consistently that its famed initials were transformed into "Clean Out of Cash and Poor Pay."

Some dramatic gesture, its operators believed, was needed to demonstrate the superiority of the central route—and win the subsidy. This they made in 1860 when they launched the Pony Express. What a glamorous paragraph in the history of transportation that was! Five hundred horses selected for their speed and stamina, stations every thirty miles where fresh mounts could be provided, tough young riders weighing less than 135 pounds willing to risk their lives by outrunning Indian attackers, for each carried only a revolver to save weight. For the sixteen months the Pony Express operated, eighty such riders were constantly in the saddle, day and night, forty flying east and forty west, carrying tissue-paper letters at ten dollars an ounce, as all the nation cheered this lightning-like conquest of space. Only ten days to cross the continent! But the Pony Express was richer in romance than profits, and its heavy losses plunged the firm of Russell, Majors and Waddell into bankruptcy. When the Civil War closed the southern route, the Butterfield Express was shifted northward to use the central route for a short time before its partners sold out to a rising coachman named Ben Holladay. Holladay dominated western stage-coaching until 1866, when he in turn disposed of his interests to a firm destined to reign during the final days of overland coaching: Wells, Fargo & Company.

Ben Holladay acted just in time, for Wells, Fargo was to win its fame not by speedy journeys across the continent, but by operating feeder lines carrying goods and passengers to a trumphant rival: the railroad. Already the iron rails were being laid that would bridge the continent; already smoke-belching locomotives were chugging westward at speeds no horse-flesh could match. Their coming heralded the dawn of a final day in the history of the frontier— a day when railroads would open all the West to the pioneers and hurry the end of westward expansion.

Closing the Frontier

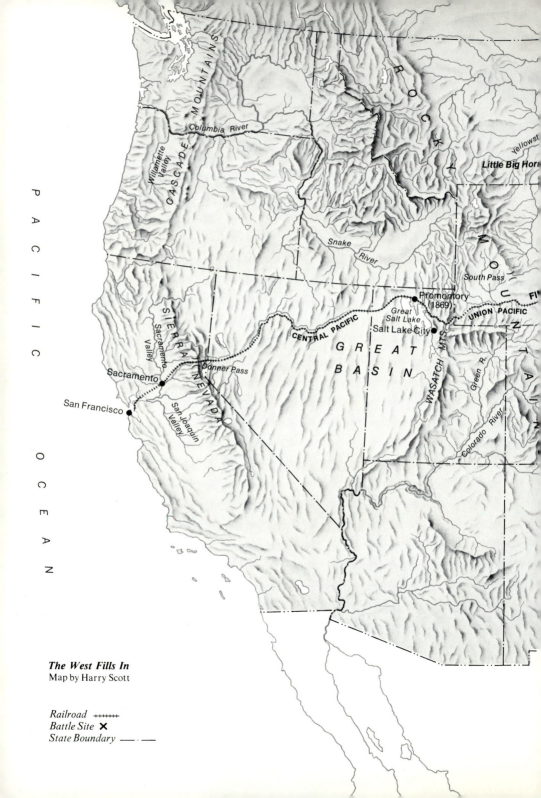

The West Fills In
Map by Harry Scott

Railroad ┼┼┼┼┼┼
Battle Site ✕
State Boundary ── ─

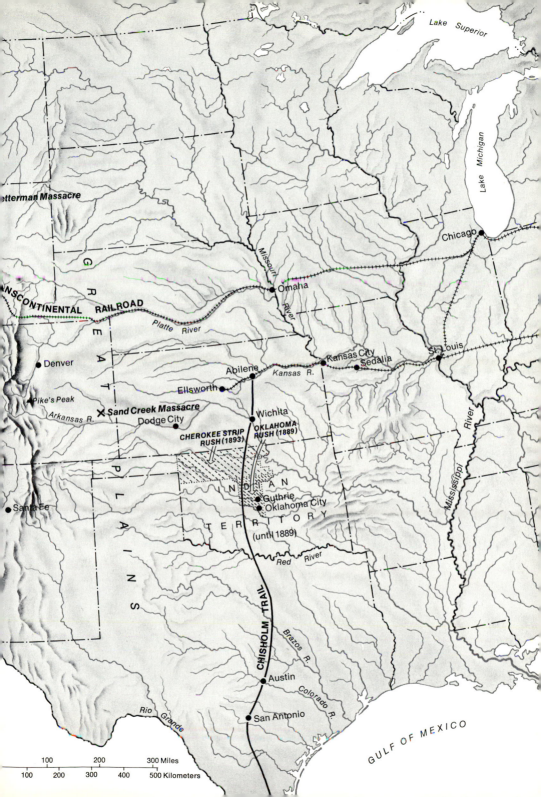

Lake Superior

Lake Michigan

etterman Massacre

G R E A T

Missouri River

Chicago

NSCONTINENTAL RAILROAD

Omaha

Platte River

Denver

Kansas City

Sedalia

St. Louis

Pike's Peak

Abilene

Kansas R.

Ellsworth

Sand Creek Massacre

Arkansas R.

Dodge City

Wichita

CHEROKEE STRIP
RUSH (1893)

OKLAHOMA
RUSH (1889)

Santa Fe

P

I N D I A N

Guthrie

Oklahoma City

Mississippi River

L

T E R R I T O R Y

(until 1889)

A

Red River

I

N

CHISHOLM TRAIL

S

Brazos R.

Austin

Colorado R.

Rio Grande

San Antonio

GULF OF MEXICO

The adventurers who leap-frogged westward to scatter their mining camps and villages across the Far West had unwittingly bypassed one of the nation's richest provinces. The Great Plains, the giant grassland stretching from western Missouri and Iowa to the Rockies, concealed more potential wealth in pasturage and farm lands than was grubbed from all the mines of western America. Yet pioneers vaulted on westward for a sensible reason: existence was impossible in a land without adequate transportation outlets, without timber for fuel and housing, and without sufficient rainfall to support normal agriculture. The inadequate water supply—generally less than the twenty inches of precipitation needed for traditional farming—was eventually to require new crops and farming methods as well as money for irrigation and well-drilling, but that could wait. The first need was for adequate transportation.

This came with the transcontinental railroads. The government subsidy necessary for such expensive projects was not forthcoming until the Confederate states left the Union at the start of the Civil War. (Northerners and Southerners had squabbled for a decade over the route the road would follow.) Then two lines were chartered, the Union Pacific to build westward from Omaha, and the Central Pacific eastward from California until they met somewhere in Utah. Federal largess—a right of way, generous land grants, and a mile-by-mile subsidy in the form of low-cost loans —touched off one of history's most frantic races, as each sought to outbuild the other to qualify for the government bounties. What a grand "Anvil Chorus" those construction crews played as they winged westward across the plains or hacked their way through the Sierra, iron ringing against iron in a symphony of sound and motion as hammers fell on spikes to bind the rails down. In May 1869 the tracks were joined at Promontory, Utah, as all the nation cheered. "The greatest triumph of modern civilization," one journalist called it; then, on second thought, "the greatest triumph of all civilization."

That triumph was to be repeated again and again over the next years as transcontinental road after transcontinental road was completed—the Kansas Pacific, the Atchison, Topeka and Santa Fe, and the Southern Pacific in the South; the Northern Pacific, Burlington Route, and Great Northern in the North

—most largely paid for by government bounties and completed by the mid-eighties. With the criss-crossing spur lines, much of the Great Plains was now available to pioneers.

But not at once, for the Indians were on the warpath. This was no commonplace struggle but the last chapter in the long, sad story of the centuries-long conflict for North America. During that warfare antagonism had sharpened and defined the purposes of each race. The Indians, weary of the fatalistic acquiescence that had allowed them to be pushed ever westward (one tribe had been moved five times from reservation to reservation) knew that they must fight or die, for they were caught between the pincers of the western-moving farm frontier and the eastern-moving mining frontier. The settlers, growing increasingly land-greedy as they sensed the vanishing of the public domain, were not sure that the red men deserved any territory useable by Americans. The governor of Colorado Territory spoke for most westerners when he declared: "I do not believe in donating to those indolent savages the best portion of my territory, and I do not believe in placing the Indians on an equality with the white man as a land holder." The red man was not capable of walking the white man's road. He must be exterminated.

These were the attitudes that explain the ferociousness of the Indian wars that broke out in the early 1860s and raged for the next thirty years. Most were bitterly fought, and marked by episodes of savage cruelty on both sides: the Chivington Massacre of 1864 where Colorado militiamen slaughtered in cold blood nearly five hundred Cheyenne and Arapaho men, women and children on the Sand Creek Reservation; the Fetterman Massacre of 1866 that cost the lives of eighty troopers on their way to relieve a transport train under attack by the Sioux; the dramatic killing of 264 troops under Lt. Col. George A. Custer—the "Longed Haired Squaw Killer," the Indians called him—at the Battle of the Little Big Horn in June 1876. Each sent a thrill of terror or exultation through the nation, but each probed the national conscience a bit deeper. Was a governmental policy that led to the slaughter of red men or white men justified? Could not some better system be found?

As federal officials groped toward a solution, one thing became clear. The Indians' traditional culture

Upper: *Cheyenne under Tall Bull tearing up Union Pacific tracks near Fossil Creek, Kansas, after driving off the track crew.* Painted by Jakob Gogolin at the direction of a survivor. Courtesy Kansas State Historical Society

Lower: *"Battle of War Bonnett Creek," (detail),* Frederic Remington. *"Was a governmental policy that led to the slaughter of red men or white men justified? Could not some better system be found?"* Courtesy Thomas Gilcrease Institute of American History and Art, Tulsa

—already doomed by the slaughter of the buffalo herds that had sustained them and their way of life— must go. Instead the red men must be "civilized"; they must settle in villages and farms, adopt the white man's ways, and eventually be absorbed into the dominant civilization. This transition could only be accomplished by herding the Indians onto reservations where they could be taught "the American way." The scattered reservations of the past would not do, for they allowed contact—and hence conflict—between the races. Instead all must be settled in the Indian Territory of modern Oklahoma. President U. S. Grant's annual message of 1872 pictured that grassland as an Eden overflowing with milk and honey where the Indians could be protected by the government until "they become sufficiently advanced in the arts of civilization to guard their own rights."

This was the policy that was heartlessly applied for the remainder of the century, as each new period of warfare was followed by the inevitable aftermath: the crowding of the defeated red men onto lands in the Indian Territory, to be theirs in perpetuity—which actually meant a few dozen years. One by one the proud tribes were transferred to new reservations, there to be educated in the white man's ways by government agents. The climax came in 1887 when the Dawes Severalty Act was passed by Congress, forcing the division of the reservations into farms to be assigned each tribal member, with the vast tracts remaining opened to white settlement. Assimilation, even by force, was the order of the day.

Fatal though that policy was to the treasured culture of the Indians, it did open the Great Plains to the frontiersmen. In the vanguard as they came flooding in were the cattlemen, eager to take advantage of free government land, easy access to eastern markets, and rising meat prices in the spawning industrialized cities of the East. Abundant cattle to stock their pastures could be had for a few dollars in Texas, where herds of wild longhorns had multiplied rapidly during the Civil War. Here were all the ingredients for a major boom, one that was to transform the plains into a giant pastureland where grass reigned as king as had cotton in the pre-war South.

The first step was to bring the beeves northward. This began in 1866 when canny Texans, aware that

86

Hugh Chee. Bishop Eatennah. Ernest Hogee.
Humphrey Escharzay. Samson Noran. Basil Ekarden.
Clement Seanilzay. Beatrice Kiahtel. Janette Pahgostatum. Margaret Y. Nadasthilah. Fred'k Eskelsejah.

Hugh Chee. Fred'k Eskelsejah. Clement Seanilzay. Samson Noran.
Ernest Hogee. Margaret Y. Nadasthilah
Humphrey Escharzay. Beatrice Kiahtel. Janette Pahgostatum. Bishop Eatennah. Basil Ekarden.

cattle worth only four or five dollars a head in the south would fetch forty or fifty dollars at the railroads then building westward, began rounding up herds for the first of the "long drives." Their destination was Sedalia, Missouri, at the head of the Missouri Pacific Railroad, but that proved an unwise choice; longhorns were unmanageable in the wooded Ozark hills and Missouri farmers came out in armed force to repel the invaders. A year later the drive shifted to Abilene, Kansas, where an Illinois meat dealer, Joseph M. McCoy, provided pens and loading chutes, and the Kansas Pacific Railroad offered favorable shipping rates. Some 1.5 million longhorns were driven over the famed Chisholm Trail to Abilene between 1867 and 1871. Then the farmers' frontier, advancing from the east, forced a shift westward, first to Ellsworth and Wichita, then to Dodge City on the Santa Fe Railroad. In all some four million cattle reached these "cattle towns" during the few years that the long drive was in its heyday.

The cattle towns (they were not labeled "cow towns" until much later, and then the term was used in a derogatory sense) have been elevated in modern films and fiction to an unenviable role as models of unbridled lawlessness. There, legend has it, the "shoot out" was a daily occurrence, stern-eyed marshals kept order by killing off a regular quota of badmen, and local boot hills received a fresh assignment of bullet-riddled corpses each hour on the hour. There, in other words, the wild, wild West was at its wildest. Andy Adams, whose semifictionalized *Log of a Cowboy* is one of the few reliable contemporary accounts of the cattle kingdom, was far more realistic when he quoted a trail-boss's warning to his crew as they were about to enter a cattle town: "Don't ever get the impression that you can ride your horses into a saloon, or shoot out the lights in Dodge. . . . You can wear your six-shooters into town, but you'd better leave them at the first place you stop, hotel, livery, or business house. And when you leave town, don't ride out shooting; omit that." Andy Adams was right; the cattle towns were run by hard-headed businessmen who knew that disorder hurt profits. They saw to it that strict regulations and an efficient police force kept criminals strictly in hand. According to actual records, in all those cattle towns between 1870 and 1885 only forty-five men were killed, and of

88

Above: *Front Street, Dodge City, Kansas. Cattle towns grew where cattle driven from Texas were loaded onto trains for the eastern markets. They were briefly booming places, but more of the bustle was about freight rates and bond issues for schools than bad men and sheriffs.* Courtesy Kansas Historical Society

Left: *Cowpens in Wichita, Kansas, about 1874.* From *The American Cowboy* (Garden City, 1973). Courtesy Harold McCracken

Above: *The great cattle drives, bringing herds from the Texas plains to the railroad in Kansas, were a remarkable part of the cattle kingdom.* Photo by Erwin E. Smith: Courtesy Mrs. L. M. Pettis and Library of Congress

Near Right: *The round-up, every boy's fantasy, was actually hot, dusty, difficult work—and still is.* Photo by Erwin E. Smith: Courtesy Mrs. L. M. Pettis and Library of Congress

these, thirty-nine died of rifle bullets or buckshot wounds, not via six-shooters.

Glamorous as were the fictionalized cattle towns and the long drives that created them, the drives were at best hazardous, and at times downright unprofitable. The longhorns lost weight on the trail, while the simultaneous arrival of a dozen herds drove the selling price downward. Far better to raise cattle near the railheads. As ranchers wakened to this economic fact, about half the herds driven northward from Texas were used to stock the plains, usually in combination with eastern breeds that improved the quality of the meat. By the 1880s cattle covered the Great Plains from Kansas to the Dakotas and westward into Montana and Wyoming, all roaming freely over the giant grassland under the watchful eyes of cowboys.

In all this gargantuan cattle kingdom scarcely a rancher owned a single foot of land. Instead his "range rights"—secured by claiming a mile or so of land along a stream—gave him absolute control of the pasture extending back to the "divide" separating his drainage basin from the next. His "rights" were protected by the live-stock association of that area; this

Opposite: *Jesse Chisholm, half-breed trader and translator (he spoke 14 Indian dialects) who traveled the Oklahoma-Texas region, translating at Indian-Army councils and doing his own trading. The wagon road he blazed from Abilene to San Antonio became the "Chisholm Trail" of cattle drive fame.* Courtesy Oklahoma Historical Society

association registered range rights and brands, supervised the semi-annual "round-ups" where cattle from neighboring herds were separated and marked, and saw to it that rustling and other activities harmful to property rights were kept at a minimum. Although operating entirely outside the law, these voluntary associations performed so efficiently that life and property were as safe on the frontier as in most eastern cities.

The true heroes of the cattle kingdom were the ranchers, but the myth-makers of that day—the newspaper reporters and novel-writers—refused to accept that simple fact. Instead they elevated the cowboy to the front rank of folk heroes: a Galahad of the Plains, splendid in sombrero and hip-hugging Levis, two revolvers worn low about his waist, blazing a path of righteousness through the West as he rescued blondes in distress or frustrated the evil designs of black-shirted villains. This image was marvelously distorted. Most cowboys found tending unruly cows an unglamorous job ("hired hands on horseback" was their favorite name for themselves) and the routine that they followed was thoroughly

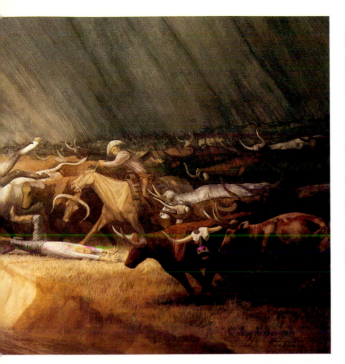

"Stampede" and "Range Burial," Harry Jackson. In the days of the open range the most dreaded danger in the cowboy's workday—or night—was the stampede. Anything could set it off: lightning, a rattlesnake, a snapped twig. Then the herd rushed mind-lessly, and often in the calm of the next day there was a lonely burial, the family far away. These magnificent paintings (10' × 21') are in the Buffalo Bill Historical Center, Cody, Wyoming, along with bronzes of the same scenes, also by Harry Jackson. Courtesy the artist and Buffalo Bill Historical Center. © Copyright Wyoming Foundry Studios, Inc., 1978

dull: "riding line" day after day to drift herds this way or that, pulling mired steers from mudholes, treating sick cows for screwworms, dreaming of the society that their solitary lives denied them. Perhaps one-third were Blacks, Mexican-Americans or Indians. Most were as likely to work in overalls, a discarded army overcoat, and a derby hat as in a ten-gallon hat and leather chaps. A good many even joined a trade union, the Knights of Labor, that struck one ranch for higher wages during the 1884 round-up.

The cowboy's place in the sun was doomed by the enormous profits of the founders of the cattle kingdom. As news of these profits spread, investors in England, Scotland, and the East poured such a torrent of capital westward that ranches multiplied beyond all reason, spilling over into marginal lands where the grass was too sparse to support herds. The cycle of moist summers and mild winters that nurtured the hopes of speculators broke in 1886-1887; that summer was so hot and dry that grass withered and died; that winter was one of bitter cold that sent thermometers tumbling to -60° and piled drifts high in the fields. Thousands upon thousands of carcasses blanketed the plains that spring, a heart-tugging reminder that humanitarian as well as financial needs required winter feeding and the fencing of the open range. Over the next years the grasslands were gradually transformed into fenced pastures, tended by cowboys who spent their days cutting hay or feeding stock rather than guiding their "cutting horses" into a milling herd at round-up time.

The days of the open range were numbered even before the disastrous winter of 1886-1887 sounded its doom, for pressing in on the cattle kingdom from the east were small farmers who were to complete the conquest of the last frontier. They resumed their march—checked for a generation by the unfamiliar environment of the Great Plains—when eastern inventors and manufacturers provided the tools that they needed. These were many: cheap barbed wire to fence their fields against cattle, windmills to raise subsurface water, well-drilling equipment, plows and harvesters and threshers that allowed a farmer to till the extensive acreage needed to support a family in that semiarid land. By 1890 a single farmer could plant and harvest 135 acres of wheat, in contrast to the 7 acres possible forty years before.

"Last of the 5,000." During the disastrous winter of 1886-87 a Montana stockman asked one of his cowboys about the condition of the herd. The cowboy, who "liked to draw," did this small sketch in reply. It gave the owner his answer, and it started the cowboy, Charles M. Russell, on his career as an artist. Courtesy Montana Stockgrowers Association

Above: *"The Rescue."* Charles Beldon owned the Pitchfork Ranch in Wyoming and his photos are a marvelous record of ranch life. Here a cowboy has rescued a blizzard-stranded calf and is moving it to some sheltered area. Courtesy Buffalo Bill Historical Center, Cody, Wyoming

Left: *"The Cowboy."* Photo by Erwin E. Smith: Courtesy Mrs. L. M. Pettis and Library of Congress

Upper: *Railroad Land Poster. Railroad builders, who had been given land as an incentive to extend their lines, realized that for them to prosper they must have settlers along the lines.* Courtesy Statue of Liberty National Monument

Lower: *Family posed in front of their first dwelling on the prairie, a dugout "soddy." The wagon, behind, holds sod for roof repairs.* Photo (1892) by Solomon D. Butcher: Courtesy Nebraska State Historical Society

At the same time an army of promoters was spreading word of the riches that awaited the pioneers on the Great Plains. Some were agents of the land-grant railroads—the transcontinental lines with 180 million acres of choice property to sell. All of these railroads set up Bureaus of Immigration that blanketed the East and Europe with advertising, arranged inspection tours, and sent an army of silver-tongued persuaders to button-hole would-be immigrants with the promise of a rags-to-riches future if they would settle in the latest Eden. Other agents were state employees, for each state and territory operated an immigration office, often in cooperation with the railroads. They were aided by the fame of the Homestead Act, passed in 1862 and trumpeted for the next half-century as the greatest boon to the working man since the invention of the wheel. "A Homestead for All" was the slogan; 160 acres of the choicest land in the world at no cost. No mention was made that speculators had already appropriated the best acreage, that the free lands usually were inferior or distant from transportation, and that 160 acres was not enough to support a family in a land where water was scarce. No matter. All the world knew that opportunity unlimited awaited the downtrodden on the Great Plains, and they came by the thousands and hundreds of thousands.

Population flowed westward along the routes of the railroads first, following the Union Pacific and Kansas Pacific and Santa Fe as far as the 100th meridian, the normal limit for the twenty inches of rainfall needed for farming, then turned northward to sweep across the Dakotas and on into Wyoming and Montana. By 1880 Kansas with 850 thousand inhabitants and Nebraska with 450 thousand were passing beyond the frontier stage; ten years later Montana and Wyoming were ready for statehood, along with South Dakota, North Dakota, Washington, and Idaho.

Those who believed the railroad advertising and expected to feast on plenty in a land of milk and honey were due for a sad awakening. Songsters might sing of the "Little Sod Shanty on the Plains" but life in a "soddy" was no bed of roses; the walls were dank and dirty, the ceiling dropped dust and straw constantly and after a rain dripped dismally for days on end. A young army bride, Alice Blackwell Baldwin, recorded her impressions when she entered the sod house near Ellsworth, Kansas, where her husband was stationed—a single chair, two empty crates, a stove stained with tobacco juice, all encrusted with the dirt that covered everything in sight, and eyeing her from the ceiling rafters a huge packrat with bushy tail held high. That was too much. She burst into tears—but the next morning she sang as she prepared breakfast and nine months later gave birth to the first baby born in Trinidad, Colorado Territory. Pioneers were made of stern stuff.

They had to be, for farming on the plains would test the stamina of a Hercules. Summer brought searing heat, winter arctic cold, the autumn deadly prairie fires, the spring occasional floods as the bank-high streams overflowed. Farmers staggered through summer day after summer day in 100° temperatures, their faces chalk-white with dried perspiration; families huddled before winter northers that plummeted thermometers to -30° with nothing to burn but dried cow dung, dried sunflower stalks, and "cats" of twisted hay. And then, like as not, a plague of grasshoppers might sweep in on the summer breeze to eat everything in sight: the crops, vegetables, bark from trees, clothes, even attacking hoe and plow handles—"everything," as one farmer put it, "but the mortgage." "Eat?" one of Hamlin Garland's characters replied to a questioner, "They wiped us out. They chawed everything that was green. They jest set around waiting f'r us to die t' eat us too." Many sodbusters surrendered to the environment and fled; after one scorching summer thirty thousand persons left Kansas for the more comfortable East. Others, their resources exhausted, had to stay singing dolefully

But here I am stuck, and here I must stay,
My money's all gone and I can't get away;
There's nothing will make a man hard and profane
Like starving to death on a government claim.

For those who persisted the rewards were great, as hundreds of thousands with the stamina and faith to stay on discovered. Gradually fields were cleared, fences built, wells dug, the sod shanty replaced with a frame house, acreage expanded—and wealth accumulated. So they came, the newcomers, from the East, from the Mississippi Valley, from Germany and Scandinavia and Russia, the eager and the hopeful

The prairie did indeed turn
out to be rich farmland, but
its rewards were reserved for
those who worked without
rest, stuck out the constant
reverses, and had luck
besides. This remarkable
"before and after" set of
pictures is the Ephraim
Swain Finches, who
homesteaded in Custer
County, Nebraska, after the
trek from Iowa, where their
parents before them had
homesteaded. Swain trapped,
ranched, and farmed as
opportunities presented
themselves; Sarah could

throw a lariat as well as
anyone, and in the early
days dealt with Indians who
usually begged, sometimes
threatened. In later years,
his success modest but solid,
"Uncle Swain" noticed the
struggles of a young
photographer who wanted to
document homestead life
before it passed. Finch
decided to sponsor him, and
the result is the magnificent
collection of Solomon D.
Butcher's photographs at the
Nebraska State Historical
Society. Finch even helped
Butcher reproduce past

scenes. Once he told the young photographer about the day the grasshoppers had come and in futile desperation he'd tried to kill the millions with a willow branch. They staged a photograph, and Butcher drew grasshoppers onto the glass negative (see photo on p. 100). The hardships had been real; successful homesteaders had reason for pride. Courtesy Nebraska State Historical Society

*The Great Plains tested her
sons sorely: loneliness was a
constant background to the
immediate threats of dust
storms* (Above) *and grasshoppers* (Right). Above:
Courtesy Library of Congress.
Right: Photo by Solomon
Butcher: Courtesy Nebraska
State Historical Society

and the displaced, to work and prosper when rainfall was plentiful, to work even harder during periodic droughts. Within two decades they had accomplished a miracle of colonization. Between 1870 and 1890 more land was occupied and more land placed under cultivation than in all the nation's previous history.

Still the land-hunger of the pioneers was not satisfied. In their midst was a fertile island not yet overrun by settlers—the Indian Territory of Oklahoma—where twenty-one tribes were crowded onto reservations guaranteed them for eternity. Why should this garden-spot of limpid streams and virgin soils be wasted on a few thousand lazy "savages" when industrious Americans could turn it into a productive wonderland? Why honor treaties made with "barbarians" when good lands for farming were nearing exhaustion? These were the questions bandied about the West as pressure mounted to open the Indian Territory to homesteaders. One part especially was demanded: a two million acre plot known as the "Oklahoma District" that had not been assigned to any tribe. Why not throw this open at once?

As petitions and resolutions descended on Congress, some frontiersmen decided to act. Early in the 1880s these "Boomers" began forming small groups to invade Oklahoma District and mark out homesteads, even though they were fully aware that their claims were illegal. Troops drove them out time after time, but the "Boomers" unwittingly accomplished what they most wanted. As exaggerated reports of their heroism—"poor, landless souls seeking a farm and cruelly treated by heartless soldiers"—blanketed the press, sympathy throughout the West and even in the East swung to their cause. Pressure on the government (liberally aided by land speculators and railroads destined to benefit) was by the end of the decade irresistible. On 23 March 1889, President Harrison announced that at noon on 22 April, just one month later, the Oklahoma District would be opened to homesteaders.

All that month the roads leading to Oklahoma were jammed with would-be settlers, most of them starry-eyed drifters who saw this as their last chance to win their share of frontier opportunity. By 22 April some one hundred thousand of them lined the borders of the district, held back by troops instructed to keep out "Sooners." Exactly at noon on that sunny day

Above: *A rare photograph of the "rush" into the "Cherokee Strip," 1893.* Courtesy Oklahoma Historical Society

Right: *The "tent city" of Guthrie, Oklahoma, after the rush. Note "Land Atty's" tent.* Courtesy Western History Collection, University of Oklahoma Library

officers fired their guns in the air and all pandemonium broke loose. Men on horseback, men in wagons, men riding bicycles, men on foot, dashed pell-mell forward amidst clouds of dust and a bedlam of noise and confusion. For the next hours the air rang with the triumphant shouts of successful "Boomers," the clatter of wagons, the crash of hammers on stakes, and the curses of disappointed homeseekers. By nightfall the Oklahoma District was settled, including Oklahoma City with a tent-dwelling population of ten thousand and Guthrie with fifteen thousand inhabitants. On 2 May 1890, the Oklahoma Territory was officially recognized by Congress.

The end was not yet, but it was coming soon. Tribe after tribe in the Indian Territory was forced to abandon its reservation in return for farms for its members, releasing vast new territories to white occupation. Each was the occasion for a new "opening" that attracted a minor "rush" of home-seekers. The most dramatic of these took place in 1893 when the six million acres of the "Cherokee Strip" were overrun in a few hours. By 1906, when an informal census showed Oklahoma with five hundred thousand inhabitants, statehood was possible; Congress admitted the new state a year later. All the West was organized now save Arizona and New Mexico which entered the Union in 1912. The political structure of the contiguous United States was completed. Forty-eight commonwealths stood as monuments to the pioneers who had carried the banners of civilization westward across the continent.

A Montana Homesteader.
Courtesy National Archives

America's Frontier Heritage

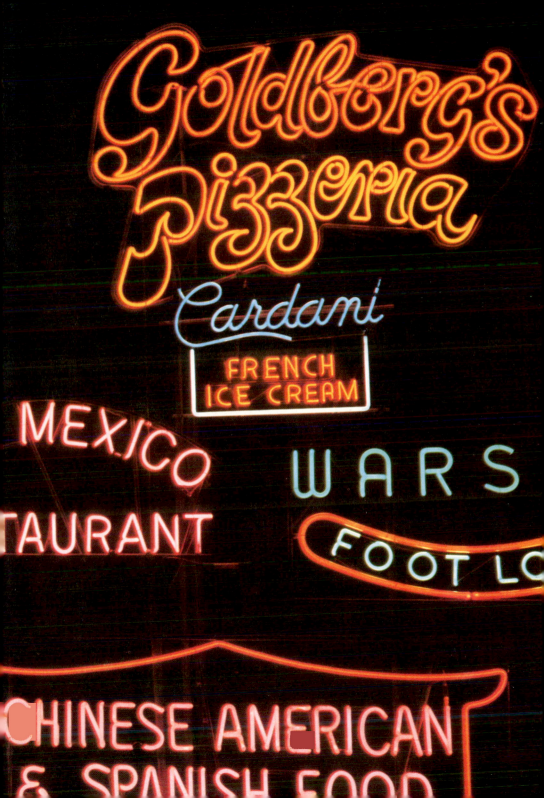

Page 104-105: *Portion of the "Nation of Nations" display, Smithsonian Institution.* Photo by Patricia Upchurch

Page 106-107: *Aerial view of Los Angeles, 1953.* Photo by William Garnett

To the American people, the rushes that symbolized the impending exhaustion of the public lands came as a shock. For generations they had been told that the supply was inexhaustible, and that westward expansion would go on for another five hundred years. Hence they were unprepared when the Superintendent of the Census announced in 1890 that the country's "unsettled area has been so broken into by isolated bodies of settlement that there can hardly be said to be a frontier line." His message, buried in an obscure public document, attracted little attention, but gradually the realization dawned that the frontier —the land of opportunity that had lured men and women westward for three centuries—would lure no more.

Actually these forebodings were decidedly premature. The West was but thinly occupied in 1890; only twice as many acres were under cultivation in the Far West as in the single state of Ohio, and even the tiny state of Delaware (which, according to its citizens, had three counties at low tide and two at high) contained more farms than Idaho or Montana, three times as many as Wyoming, and seven times as many as Arizona. There still was room along the frontiers for newcomers; there still was opportunity for the dispossessed to "grow up with the country."

So the migration continued, as the "westward tilt" of the continent spilled the adventuresome and the ambitious toward the setting sun. Four times as many acres were homesteaded in the West after 1890 as before, and twice as many have been since 1910 as in the prior fifty years. The persistence of the movement was also revealed by the regular shift westward of the center of population, from central Indiana in 1890 to the village of Mascoutah in Illinois' St. Clair County in 1970. During those years, too, those unable to find land in the American West turned northward toward Canada's open spaces; between 1900 and 1920 some three hundred thousand left the United States for farms in Manitoba, Alberta and Saskatchewan. The "last, best West" was still attracting, and the westward movement still helping shape the nation's economy and culture.

This migration softened the impact of the exhaustion of the public domain, but it could not hide the fact that the frontier movement was passing into history. As this realization slowly dawned, thinking

Americans faced a series of troublesome questions. Could farmers long accustomed to land-exploitation adjust themselves to European habits of conservation? Could workers who (most economists believed) had maintained the world's highest living standard by dumping excess laborers on the frontier during crisis periods, accept increasing competition and lower wages? Would "radicals" demand destructive social reforms now that the discontented could no longer escape through the "safety valve" of the West? Could a people whose traditions and institutions had been formulated in an age of expansion adjust to a stable society? And, most important of all, could the democracy that had been nurtured by frontier opportunity survive in a closed-space nation?

The United States has been seeking answers to those questions for more than three-quarters of a century. Most of its leaders have recognized that the dog-eat-dog economy of the nineteenth century has been outmoded by the frontier's passing, and that cooperation rather than unrestricted competition must be the order of the future. They have also seen that only the federal government has sufficient power and resources to provide the people with the security and opportunity formerly provided by cheap land, and to serve as a watchdog over society in an era of increasing competition for dwindling natural resources. If this requires a more positive role on the part of the president and Congress, with a corresponding lessening of individual freedom, so be it. The passing of the frontier and the coming of the machine age have made the change imperative.

This is the reasoning that has shaped the political beliefs of progressive Americans since the dawn of the twentieth century. Theodore Roosevelt's "Square Deal" was rooted in the belief that the vanishing natural resources must be protected and equitably allotted; Woodrow Wilson's "New Freedom" sought to insure individual opportunity by checking industrial monopoly; Franklin D. Roosevelt's "New Deal," John F. Kennedy's "New Frontier," and Lyndon B. Johnson's "Great Society" all were based on the realization that the state must care for a variety of needs formerly satisfied by the opportunity to flee westward. Implementing these beliefs has been the purpose of most of the important legislative programs of the twentieth century, from laws aimed at the conservation of natural resources, to those providing social security and medical aid.

Just as the frontier's closing has altered the nation's political climate, so has it effected American behavior. The aspects of the national character most closely linked with frontier opportunity—the migratory compulsion, inventive inclination, rose-tinted optimism, excessive wastefulness, strong work ethic, a unique social democracy—have during the last half-century gradually adjusted to the needs of a closed-space industrial-urban environment. Traits most closely linked to rural life have eroded most rapidly, others more slowly.

Thus the inventive urge remains strong and the patent office as busy as usual; technological improvement challenges the ingenuity of creative individuals just as the unique problems posed by expansion did. Similarly social democracy—a fundamental faith in equality—has persisted (save among minorities denied their proper place on the national escalator), even though the rags-to-riches fable on which it rested in the past is less widely believed. Today industrial opportunity opens the path to upward mobility for the industrious and talented, just as frontier opportunity did in the past. Hence class lines are less rigidly drawn in the United States than in European countries more steeped in tradition. The taxicab driver who calls his well-dressed customer "Mac" rather than "Sir" is responding to a frontier tradition that saw all men as potentially equal, and to be treated as such.

Americans also remain the most migratory of all western-world peoples, for transportation improvements give free vent to the wandering tendencies learned from our pioneer ancestors. We are eternally on the move—"permanently transitory" as one observer noted. We Americans live in automobiles, pausing in our eternal flight now and then at drive-in theaters, or drive-in restaurants, or drive-in banks, or "Park-and-Pray" churches. Some of us are forever on wheels, carrying our homes about with us like turtles; in the 1970s more than 750 thousand motor homes and trailers roamed the highways. We also shift about with alarming regularity; each year some thirty-six million of us move from one spot to another within the county where we live and another fifteen million shift from one county to another. So often do we move that bank statements, magazines and even

Part of more than 2,000 travel trailers at a convention in Las Cruces, New Mexico, June 1979. Photo by Bob Sigmon: Courtesy Las Cruces Sun-News

dividend checks regularly include change-of-address slips. "If," wrote a Latin American visitor not long ago, "God were suddenly to call the world to judgment, He would surprise two-thirds of the Americans on the road, like ants."

The habit of wastefulness has proved equally hard to break. Conservationists have preached the necessity of preserving natural resources since the dawn of the twentieth century, bolstering their pleas with statistics to prove that the forests, fuel, minerals and soils of the United States would be exhausted within generations. These pleas have been met with bland indifference by most of the people, even after the energy crisis of the mid-1970s dramatically demonstrated that the United States lacks enough fossil fuels to satisfy its needs. Statisticians and politicians might urge saving, and a growing army of "environmentalists" might cry doom, but the majority refuses to listen. That 55 mph speed limit simply does not apply to anyone in a hurry (and what American is not, even when he has no place to go?). Besides, the old bus runs better at 65 than at 55. So we Americans have gone on squandering our birthright just as did our pioneer ancestors; the United States to Europeans is the land of the no-deposit-no-return bottle, the disposable tissue, the throw-away beer can, the bag-within-the-bag-within-the-bag at the supermarket. We still cling to a frontier-like faith that the future will provide, whatever the evidence to the contrary.

The work ethic that possessed pioneers has lost force, but its shadow remains. Today, with machines doing much of the drudgery formerly required of man, Americans still labor longer and harder than their cousins in older countries. We can find no time in our busy lives for the leisurely tea that is a treasured tradition in England, the restful siesta that soothes the Latin temperament, the unhurried lingering over a glass of wine in a sidewalk cafe that gladdens life in Paris or Rome. Only recently have the coffee-break, the two-martini lunch, and the interest in a shorter work week threatened the unending drive of middle-class America toward heart attacks and stomach ulcers. Even the one acceptable period of leisure—the cocktail hour—requires the consumption of liquids of such persuasive intensity that the maximum degree of rejuvenation is achieved in the minimum amount of time.

Strip mining: the cheapest way to get at much of our remaining energy resources, and a classic confrontation of conflicting ethics. Photo by Nick Decker: Courtesy Missouri Department of Natural Resources

These are but symptoms of a changing national temperament that has manifested itself since the exhaustion of the government domain closed the door on frontier opportunity. The full shock of the frontier's closing has yet to be felt, and perhaps never will be if Yankee ingenuity and wise leadership develop substitutes for cheap lands. These could be in the form of sufficient energy to fuel continuing expansion of the economy, and wisely administered governmental programs to assure all people security and opportunity. If these things can be done, Americans may continue to enjoy the abundance, the freedom, and the opportunity for self-advancement that have been the frontier's principal contribution to the success of the Republic.

"The Old Stagecoach,"
Eastman Johnson. Courtesy
Milwaukee Art Center,
Layton Art Collection